INTERNATIONAL GCSE

English Anthology

ANTHOLOGY

Pearson Edexcel International GCSE English Anthology for use with:

Edexcel International GCSE in English Literature (4ET1)

Edexcel International GCSE in English Language (Specification A) (4EA1)

ALWAYS LEARNING   **PEARSON**

Published by Pearson Education Limited, 80 Strand, London, WC2R 0RL.

Copies of official specifications for all Edexcel qualifications may be found on the website: qualifications.pearson.com

© Pearson Education Limited 2016

First published 2016

19 18 17 16

10 9 8 7 6 5 4 3 2 1

British Library Cataloguing in Publication Data

A catalogue record for this book is available from the British Library.

ISBN 978 1 446 93632 0

Contents

Part 3: Paper 1 Section A Poetry

Introduction

This anthology has been prepared to support the following specifications:

- Pearson Edexcel International GCSE (9-1) in English Language (Specification A)
- Pearson Edexcel International GCSE (9-1) in English Literature.

International GCSE (9-1) in English Language (Specification A)

Students studying the English Language (Specification A) qualification must study all the English Language non-fiction texts in this anthology in preparation for Paper 1 Section A of the examination. Students will be asked to analyse an anthology text and compare it to an unseen non-fiction piece. Copies of the anthology must not be taken into the examination. The anthology text, along with the unseen text, will be printed in an Extracts Booklet, which will accompany the question paper.

For both examined and coursework options, students must study all the English Language poetry and prose texts in the anthology for Paper 2 (examined) and Paper 3 (coursework) of the qualification.

Students taking the full examination route will be asked to analyse a poetry or prose anthology text (Paper 2 Section A), which will be printed in the question paper.

Students taking the coursework route will be asked to write an analytical essay, exploring a topic of their choice on two poetry or prose anthology texts. This is accompanied by a short commentary explaining why the student has chosen their texts.

Further information is given in the specification, which must be read in conjunction with this anthology.

International GCSE (9-1) in English Literature

Students studying the English Literature qualification must study all the English Literature poems in preparation for Paper 1 Section A of the examination.

Students will be asked to compare two anthology poems from a choice of two questions. A booklet containing all the English Literature poems will be provided with the examination paper.

International GCSE English Language (Specification A)

Part 1: Paper 1 Section A Non-fiction texts

(handwritten: main argument)

(handwritten: (metaphor) Shows about stereotypes)

From *The Danger of a Single Story*, Chimamanda Ngozi Adichie

(handwritten: 15099955 views)

Adichie, a successful novelist, delivered this speech at a TED conference. She speaks about the power of storytelling and the danger of a single view.

(handwritten: (Anecdotal)) *(handwritten: (Rhetorical device) ethos, pathos, logos)*

(handwritten: (personal pronoun)) *(handwritten: (Cautionary tone))*

I'm a storyteller. And I would like to tell you a few personal stories about what I like to call "the danger of the single story." I grew up on a university campus in eastern Nigeria. My mother says that I started reading at the age of two, although I think four is probably close to the truth. So I was an early reader, and what I read were British and

5 American children's books.

(handwritten: (ethos) makes audience listen to her carefully. more accurate)

I was also an early writer, and when I began to write, at about the age of seven, stories in pencil with crayon illustrations that my poor mother was obligated to read, I wrote exactly the kinds of stories I was reading: all my characters were white and blue-eyed, they played in the snow, they ate apples, and they talked a lot about the weather, how

10 lovely it was that the sun had come out.

(handwritten: (pathos) humor)

(handwritten: (Juxtaposition) Shows how different was her compared with stories that she read)

(handwritten: Listing: monotony, uninspiring)

Now, this despite the fact that I lived in Nigeria. I had never been outside Nigeria. We didn't have snow, we ate mangoes, and we never talked about the weather, because there was no need to. …

(handwritten: direct opposite) *(handwritten: (collective pronoun))*

(handwritten: (Emotive language) want audience to know about how bad)

(handwritten: 印象的的; 脆弱的)

What this demonstrates, I think, is how impressionable and vulnerable we are in the face

15 of a story, particularly as children. Because all I had read were books in which characters were foreign, I had become convinced that books by their very nature had to have foreigners in them and had to be about things with which I could not personally identify. Now, things changed when I discovered African books. There weren't many of them available, and they weren't quite as easy to find as the foreign books.

(handwritten: (Ethos) credibility)

20 But because of writers like Chinua Achebe and Camara Laye, I went through a mental shift in my perception of literature. I realized that people like me, girls with skin the colour of chocolate, whose kinky hair could not form ponytails, could also exist in literature. I started to write about things I recognized.

(handwritten: (Empathetic Tone) don't want to blame anyone)

(handwritten: (complimentary) don't want to blame any audience)

Now, I loved those American and British books I read. They stirred my imagination. They

25 opened up new worlds for me. But the unintended consequence was that I did not know that people like me could exist in literature. So what the discovery of African writers did for me was this: It saved me from having a single story of what books are.

(handwritten: Draws importance in following clause.) *(handwritten: contrast to the danger of a single story.)*

(handwritten: (Logos) Share experience: She had a single story of Fide)

I come from a conventional, middle-class Nigerian family. My father was a professor. My

30 mother was an administrator. And so we had, as was the norm, live-in domestic help, who would often come from nearby rural villages. So, the year I turned eight, we got a new house boy. His name was Fide. The only thing my mother told us about him was that his family was very poor. My mother sent yams and rice, and our old clothes, to his family. And when I didn't finish my dinner, my mother would say, "Finish your food! Don't you know? People like Fide's family have nothing." So I felt enormous pity for

35 Fide's family.

(handwritten: (pathos) humor)

(handwritten: Time expressions)

Then one Saturday, we went to his village to visit, and his mother showed us a beautifully patterned basket made of dyed raffia that his brother had made. I was startled. It had not occurred to me that anybody in his family could actually make something. All I had heard about them was how poor they were, so that it had become

40 impossible for me to see them as anything else but poor. Their poverty was my single story of them.

(handwritten: (Logos) critiques herself)

Years later, I thought about this when I left Nigeria to go to university in the United States. I was 19. My American roommate was shocked by me. She asked where I had learned to speak English so well, and was confused when I said that Nigeria happened to

45 have English as its official language. She asked if she could listen to what she called my

Pearson Edexcel International GCSE English Anthology
Issue 1 — April 2016 © Pearson Education Limited 2016

"tribal music", and was consequently very disappointed when I produced my tape of Mariah Carey. *→ reference to popular culture Contrast. (humor)*

She assumed that I did not know how to use a stove. *(short sentence) = limited view*

50 What struck me was this: She had felt sorry for me even before she saw me. Her default position toward me, as an African, was a kind of patronizing, well-meaning pity. My roommate had a single story of Africa: a single story of catastrophe. In this single story, there was no possibility of Africans being similar to her in any way, no possibility of feelings more complex than pity, no possibility of a connection as human equals. ...

(parallel sentence structure) *limited view*

(Empathetic tone) shows her roommate wasn't mean to. Anaphora

55 So, after I had spent some years in the U.S. as an African, I began to understand my roommate's response to me. If I had not grown up in Nigeria, and if all I knew about Africa were from popular images, I too would think that Africa was a place of beautiful landscapes, beautiful animals, and incomprehensible people, fighting senseless wars, dying of poverty and AIDS, unable to speak for themselves and waiting to be saved by a kind, white foreigner. I would see Africans in the same way that I, as a child, had seen

60 Fide's family. ... *→ draws parallels between herself and her roommate = empathetic tone → Critiques herself*

Logos shows her experience (Fide's family) how difficult it is.

But I must quickly add that I too am just as guilty in the question of the single story. A few years ago, I visited Mexico from the U.S. The political climate in the U.S. at the time was tense, and there were debates going on about immigration. And, as often happens in America, immigration became synonymous with Mexicans. There were endless stories

65 of Mexicans as people who were fleecing the healthcare system, sneaking across the border, being arrested at the border, that sort of thing. *→ (Dismissive tone)*

negative images

(language choice)

contrast

I remember walking around on my first day in Guadalajara, watching the people going to work, rolling up tortillas in the marketplace, smoking, laughing. I remember first feeling slight surprise. And then, I was overwhelmed with shame. I realized that I had been so

70 immersed in the media coverage of Mexicans that they had become one thing in my mind, the abject immigrant. I had bought into the single story of Mexicans and I could not have been more ashamed of myself. *★ She also had a single story of Mexicans ★ She ashamed herself a lot.*

positive image

↓ lack of conjunction

Repetition (emphasizes a lot)

So that is how to create a single story, show a people as one thing, as only one thing, over and over again, and that is what they become. ... *repetition*

75 Stories matter. Many stories matter. Stories have been used to dispossess and to malign, but stories can also be used to empower and to humanize. Stories can break the dignity of a people, but stories can also repair that broken dignity.

The American writer Alice Walker wrote this about her Southern relatives who had moved to the North. She introduced them to a book about the Southern life that they

80 had left behind. "They sat around, reading the book themselves, listening to me read the book, and a kind of paradise was regained."

I would like to end with this thought: That when we reject the single story, when we realize that there is never a single story about any place, we regain a kind of paradise.

- the single story creates stereotypes.
- the problem of stereotypes is not that they are untrue.
- but that they are incomplete → is not all mexicans

From *A Passage to Africa*, George Alagiah

Alagiah writes about his experiences as a television reporter during the war in Somalia, Africa in the 1990s. He won a special award for his report on the incidents described in this passage.

I saw a thousand hungry, lean, scared and betrayed faces as I criss-crossed Somalia between the end of 1991 and December 1992, but there is one I will never forget.

I was in a little hamlet just outside Gufgaduud, a village in the back of beyond, a place the aid agencies had yet to reach. In my notebook I had jotted down instructions on how
5   to get there. 'Take the Badale Road for a few kilometres till the end of the tarmac, turn right on to a dirt track, stay on it for about forty-five minutes — Gufgaduud. Go another fifteen minutes approx. — like a ghost village.' ...

In the ghoulish manner of journalists on the hunt for the most striking pictures, my cameraman ... and I tramped from one hut to another. What might have appalled us
10   when we'd started our trip just a few days before no longer impressed us much. The search for the shocking is like the craving for a drug: you require heavier and more frequent doses the longer you're at it. Pictures that stun the editors one day are written off as the same old stuff the next. This sounds callous, but it is just a fact of life. It's how we collect and compile the images that so move people in the comfort of their sitting
15   rooms back home.

There was Amina Abdirahman, who had gone out that morning in search of wild, edible roots, leaving her two young girls lying on the dirt floor of their hut. They had been sick for days, and were reaching the final, enervating stages of terminal hunger. Habiba was ten years old and her sister, Ayaan, was nine. By the time Amina returned, she had only
20   one daughter. Habiba had died. No rage, no whimpering, just a passing away — that simple, frictionless, motionless deliverance from a state of half-life to death itself. It was, as I said at the time in my dispatch, a vision of 'famine away from the headlines, a famine of quiet suffering and lonely death'.

There was the old woman who lay in her hut, abandoned by relations who were too weak
25   to carry her on their journey to find food. It was the smell that drew me to her doorway: the smell of decaying flesh. Where her shinbone should have been there was a festering wound the size of my hand. She'd been shot in the leg as the retreating army of the deposed dictator ... took revenge on whoever it found in its way. The shattered leg had fused into the gentle V-shape of a boomerang. It was rotting; she was rotting. You could
30   see it in her sick, yellow eyes and smell it in the putrid air she recycled with every struggling breath she took.

And then there was the face I will never forget.

My reaction to everyone else I met that day was a mixture of pity and revulsion[1]. Yes, revulsion. The degeneration of the human body, sucked of its natural vitality by the twin
35   evils of hunger and disease, is a disgusting thing. We never say so in our TV reports. It's a taboo that has yet to be breached. To be in a feeding centre is to hear and smell the excretion of fluids by people who are beyond controlling their bodily functions. To be in a feeding centre is surreptitiously[2] to wipe your hands on the back of your trousers after you've held the clammy palm of a mother who has just cleaned vomit from her child's
40   mouth.

There's pity, too, because even in this state of utter despair they aspire to a dignity that is almost impossible to achieve. An old woman will cover her shrivelled body with a

---

[1] *revulsion*: disgust
[2] *surreptitiously*: secretly

Pearson Edexcel International GCSE English Anthology
Issue 1 — April 2016 © Pearson Education Limited 2016

soiled cloth as your gaze turns towards her. Or the old and dying man who keeps his hoe next to the mat with which, one day soon, they will shroud his corpse, as if he means to
45   go out and till the soil once all this is over.

I saw that face for only a few seconds, a fleeting meeting of eyes before the face turned away, as its owner retreated into the darkness of another hut. In those brief moments there had been a smile, not from me, but from the face. It was not a smile of greeting, it was not a smile of joy — how could it be? — but it was a smile nonetheless. It touched
50   me in a way I could not explain. It moved me in a way that went beyond pity or revulsion.

What was it about that smile? I had to find out. I urged my translator to ask the man why he had smiled. He came back with an answer. 'It's just that he was embarrassed to be found in this condition,' the translator explained. And then it clicked. That's what the
55   smile had been about. It was the feeble smile that goes with apology, the kind of smile you might give if you felt you had done something wrong.

Normally inured[3] to stories of suffering, accustomed to the evidence of deprivation, I was unsettled by this one smile in a way I had never been before. There is an unwritten code between the journalist and his subjects in these situations. The journalist observes, the
60   subject is observed. The journalist is active, the subject is passive. But this smile had turned the tables on that tacit agreement. Without uttering a single word, the man had posed a question that cut to the heart of the relationship between me and him, between us and them, between the rich world and the poor world. If he was embarrassed to be found weakened by hunger and ground down by conflict, how should I feel to be
65   standing there so strong and confident?

I resolved there and then that I would write the story of Gufgaduud with all the power and purpose I could muster. It seemed at the time, and still does, the only adequate answer a reporter can give to the man's question.

I have one regret about that brief encounter in Gufgaduud. Having searched through my
70   notes and studied the dispatch that the BBC broadcast, I see that I never found out what the man's name was. Yet meeting him was a seminal moment in the gradual collection of experiences we call context. Facts and figures are the easy part of journalism. Knowing where they sit in the great scheme of things is much harder. So, my nameless friend, if you are still alive, I owe you one.

---

[3] *inured*: hardened

From *The Explorer's Daughter*, Kari Herbert

As a small child, Herbert lived, with her family, among the Inughuit people (sometimes called Inuits, or Eskimos) in the harsh environment of the Arctic. In 2002 she revisited the area, staying near Thule, a remote settlement in North Greenland. In this passage she writes about her experience of watching a hunt for the narwhal, a toothed whale, and what she thought and felt about it.

Two hours after the last of the hunters had returned and eaten, narwhal were spotted again, this time very close. Within an hour even those of us on shore could with the naked eye see the plumes of spray from the narwhal catching the light in a spectral play of colour. Two large pods[1] of narwhal circled in the fjord[2], often looking as if they were
5 going to merge, but always slowly, methodically passing each other by. Scrambling back up to the lookout I looked across the glittering kingdom in front of me and took a sharp intake of breath. The hunters were dotted all around the fjord. The evening light was turning butter-gold, glinting off man and whale and catching the soft billows of smoke from a lone hunter's pipe. From where we sat at the lookout it looked as though the
10 hunters were close enough to touch the narwhal with their bare hands and yet they never moved. Distances are always deceptive in the Arctic, and I fell to wondering if the narwhal existed at all or were instead mischievous tricks of the shifting light. …

The narwhal rarely stray from High Arctic waters, escaping only to the slightly more temperate waters towards the Arctic Circle in the dead of winter, but never entering the
15 warmer southern seas. In summer the hunters of Thule are fortunate to witness the annual return of the narwhal to the Inglefield Fjord, on the side of which we now sat.

The narwhal … is an essential contributor to the survival of the hunters in the High Arctic. The mattak or blubber[3] of the whale is rich in necessary minerals and vitamins, and in a place where the climate prohibits the growth of vegetables or fruit, this rich
20 source of vitamin C was the one reason that the Eskimos have never suffered from scurvy[4]. … For centuries the blubber of the whales was also the only source of light and heat, and the dark rich meat is still a valuable part of the diet for both man and dogs (a single narwhal can feed a team of dogs for an entire month). Its single ivory tusk, which can grow up to six feet in length, was used for harpoon tips and handles for other
25 hunting implements (although the ivory was found to be brittle and not hugely satisfactory as a weapon), for carving protective tupilaks[5], and even as a central beam for their small ancient dwellings. Strangely, the tusk seems to have little use for the narwhal itself; they do not use the tusk to break through ice as a breathing hole, nor will they use it to catch or attack prey, but rather the primary use seems to be to disturb the
30 top of the sea bed in order to catch Arctic halibut for which they have a particular predilection[6]. Often the ends of their tusks are worn down or even broken from such usage.

The women clustered on the knoll of the lookout, binoculars pointing in every direction, each woman focusing on her husband or family member, occasionally spinning round at
35 a small gasp or jump as one of the women saw a hunter near a narwhal. … Each wife knew her husband instinctively and watched their progress intently; it was crucial to her that her husband catch a narwhal — it was part of their staple diet, and some of the

---

[1] *pods*: small groups of whales
[2] *fjord*: a long, narrow inlet of the sea with steep sides
[3] *mattak* or blubber: the fatty skin of the whale
[4] *scurvy*: a painful, weakening disease caused by a lack of vitamin C
[5] *tupilaks*: figures with magical powers, charms
[6] *predilection*: liking

Pearson Edexcel International GCSE English Anthology
Issue 1 — April 2016 © Pearson Education Limited 2016

mattak and meat could be sold to other hunters who hadn't been so lucky, bringing in some much-needed extra income. Every hunter was on the water. It was like watching a
40 vast, waterborne game with the hunters spread like a net around the sound.

The narwhal … are intelligent creatures, their senses are keen and they talk to one another under the water. Their hearing is particularly developed and they can hear the sound of a paddling kayak from a great distance. That … was why the hunters had to sit so very still in the water.

45 One hunter was almost on top of a pair of narwhal, and they were huge. He gently picked up his harpoon and aimed — in that split second my heart leapt for both hunter and narwhal. I urged the man on in my head; he was so close, and so brave to attempt what he was about to do — he was miles from land in a flimsy kayak, and could easily be capsized and drowned. The hunter had no rifle, only one harpoon with two heads and
50 one bladder. It was a foolhardy exercise and one that could only inspire respect. And yet at the same time my heart also urged the narwhal to dive, to leave, to survive.

This dilemma stayed with me the whole time that I was in Greenland. I understand the harshness of life in the Arctic and the needs of the hunters and their families to hunt and live on animals and sea mammals that we demand to be protected because of their
55 beauty. And I know that one cannot afford to be sentimental in the Arctic. 'How can you possibly eat seal?' I have been asked over and over again. True, the images that bombarded us several years ago of men battering seals for their fur hasn't helped the issue of polar hunting, but the Inughuit do not kill seals using this method, nor do they kill for sport. They use every part of the animals they kill, and most of the food in Thule
60 is still brought in by the hunter-gatherers and fishermen. Imported goods can only ever account for part of the food supply; there is still only one annual supply ship that makes it through the ice to Qaanaaq, and the small twice-weekly plane from West Greenland can only carry a certain amount of goods. Hunting is still an absolute necessity in Thule.

***Explorers or boys messing about? Either way, taxpayer gets rescue bill*, Steven Morris**

Adapted from an article published in *The Guardian* newspaper, 28 January 2003. Helicopter duo plucked from liferaft after Antarctic crash

Their last expedition ended in <u>farce</u> when the Russians threatened to send in military planes to intercept them as they tried to cross into Siberia via the icebound Bering Strait.

5 Yesterday a new adventure undertaken by British explorers Steve Brooks and Quentin Smith almost led to <u>tragedy</u> when their helicopter plunged into the sea off Antarctica.

The men were plucked from the icy water by a Chilean naval ship after a nine-hour rescue which began when Mr Brooks contacted his wife, Jo Vestey, on his satellite phone asking for assistance. The rescue involved the Royal Navy, the RAF and British coastguards.

10 Last night there was <u>resentment</u> in some quarters that the men's adventure had cost the taxpayers of Britain and Chile tens of thousands of pounds. *[anger and upset]*

Experts questioned the wisdom of taking a small helicopter — the four-seater Robinson R44 has a single engine — into such a hostile environment.

There was also confusion about what exactly the men were trying to achieve. A website
15 set up to promote the Bering Strait expedition claims the team were planning to fly from the north to south pole in their "<u>trusty helicopter</u>". *[ironic statement]*

[another perspectives] But Ms Vestey claimed she did not know what the pair were up to, describing them as '<u>boys</u> messing about with a helicopter'.

The drama began at around 1am British time when Mr Brooks, <u>42</u>, and <u>40-year-old</u> Mr
20 Smith, also known as <u>Q</u>, ditched into the sea 100 miles off Antarctica, about 36 miles north of Smith Island, and scrambled into their liferaft.

Mr Brooks called his wife in London on his satellite phone. She said: 'He said they were both in the liferaft but were okay and could I call the <u>emergency people</u>?' *[inexperienced]*

Meanwhile, distress signals were being beamed from the ditched helicopter and from Mr
25 Brooks' Breitling emergency watch, a wedding present.

[Reassuring] The signals from the aircraft were <u>deciphered</u> by Falmouth[1] coastguard and passed on to the rescue coordination centre at RAF Kinloss in Scotland. *[decision]*

The Royal Navy's ice patrol ship, HMS Endurance, which was 180 miles away <u>surveying</u> *[exploring more]* uncharted waters, began steaming towards the scene and dispatched its two Lynx
30 helicopters.

One was driven back because of poor visibility but the second was on its way when the men were picked up by a Chilean naval vessel at about 10.20am British time.

Though the pair wore survival suits and the weather at the spot where they ditched was clear, one Antarctic explorer told Mr Brooks' wife it was 'nothing short of a miracle' that
35 they had survived.

Both men are experienced adventurers. Mr Brooks, a property developer from London, has taken part in expeditions to 70 countries in 15 years. He has trekked solo to Everest base camp and walked barefoot for three days in the Himalayas. He has negotiated the

---

[1] *Falmouth*: a coastal town in Cornwall, England

40 white water rapids of the Zambezi river by kayak and survived a charge by a silver back gorilla in the Congo. He is also a qualified mechanical engineer and pilot.

He and his wife spent their honeymoon flying the helicopter from Alaska to Chile. The 16,000-mile trip took three months.

Mr Smith, also from London, claims to have been flying since the age of five. He has twice flown a helicopter around the globe and won the world freestyle helicopter flying
45 championship.

Despite their experience, it is not the first time they have hit the headlines for the wrong reasons.

In April, Mr Brooks and another explorer, Graham Stratford, were poised to become the first to complete a crossing of the 56-mile wide frozen Bering Strait between the US and
50 Russia in an amphibious vehicle, Snowbird VI, which could carve its way through ice floes and float in the water in between.

But they were forced to call a halt after the Russian authorities told them they would scramble military helicopters to lift them off the ice if they crossed the border.

Ironically, one of the aims of the expedition, for which Mr Smith provided air back-up,
55 was to demonstrate how good relations between east and west had become.

The wisdom of the team's latest adventure was questioned by, among others, Günter Endres, editor of Jane's Helicopter Markets and Systems, said: 'I'm surprised they used the R44. I wouldn't use a helicopter like that to go so far over the sea. It sounds as if they were pushing it to the maximum'.

60 A spokesman for the pair said it was not known what had gone wrong. The flying conditions had been 'excellent'.

The Ministry of Defence said the taxpayer would pick up the bill, as was normal in rescues in the UK and abroad. The spokesperson said it was 'highly unlikely' it would recover any of the money.

65 Last night the men were on their way to the Chilean naval base Eduardo Frei, where HMS Endurance was to pick them up. Ms Vestey said: 'They have been checked and appear to be well. I don't know what will happen to them once they have been picked up by HMS Endurance — they'll probably have their bottoms kicked and be sent home the long way'.

From _Between a Rock and a Hard Place_, Aron Ralston

In this first-hand account, Ralston describes how a boulder crushed his right hand while he was climbing and hiking in a canyon. He had not informed anyone of his hiking plans.

I come to another drop-off. This one is maybe eleven or twelve feet high, a foot higher and of a different geometry than the overhang I descended ten minutes ago. Another refrigerator chockstone[1] is wedged between the walls, ten feet downstream from and at the same height as the ledge. It gives the space below the drop-off the claustrophobic

5 feel of a short tunnel. Instead of the walls widening after the drop-off, or opening into a bowl at the bottom of the canyon, here the slot narrows to a consistent three feet across at the lip of the drop-off and continues at that width for fifty feet down the canyon.

Sometimes in narrow passages like this one, it's possible for me to stem my body across the slot, with my feet and back pushing out in opposite directions against the walls.

10 Controlling this counterpressure by switching my hands and feet on the opposing walls, I can move up or down the shoulder-width crevice fairly easily as long as the friction contact stays solid between the walls and my hands, feet, and back. This technique is known as stemming or chimneying; you can imagine using it to climb up the inside of a chimney.

15 Just below the ledge where I'm standing is a chockstone the size of a large bus tire[2], stuck fast in the channel between the walls, a few feet out from the lip. If I can step onto it, then I'll have a nine-foot height to descend, less than that of the first overhang. I'll dangle off the chockstone, then take a short fall onto the rounded rocks piled on the canyon floor.

20 Stemming across the canyon at the lip of the drop-off, with one foot and one hand on each of the walls, I traverse[3] out to the chockstone. I press my back against the south wall and lock my left knee, which pushes my foot tight against the north wall. With my right foot, I kick at the boulder to test how stuck it is. It's jammed tightly enough to hold my weight. I lower myself from the chimneying position and step onto the chockstone. It

25 supports me but teeters slightly. After confirming that I don't want to chimney down from the chockstone's height, I squat and grip the rear of the lodged boulder, turning to face back upcanyon. Sliding my belly over the front edge, I can lower myself and hang from my fully extended arms, akin to climbing down from the roof of a house.

As I dangle, I feel the stone respond to my adjusting grip with a scraping quake as my

30 body's weight applies enough torque[4] to disturb it from its position. Instantly, I know this is trouble, and instinctively, I let go of the rotating boulder to land on the round rocks below. When I look up, the backlit chockstone falling toward my head consumes the sky. Fear shoots my hands over my head. I can't move backward or I'll fall over a small ledge. My only hope is to push off the falling rock and get my head out of its way.

35 The next three seconds play out at a tenth of their normal speed. Time dilates, as if I'm dreaming, and my reactions decelerate. In slow motion: the rock smashes my left hand against the south wall; my eyes register the collision, and I yank my left arm back as the rock ricochets[5]; the boulder then crushes my right hand and ensnares my right arm at the wrist, palm in, thumb up, fingers extended; the rock slides another foot down the

---

[1] _chockstone_: a stone that has become wedged between rocks
[2] _tire_: American spelling of tyre
[3] _traverse_: cross
[4] _torque_: rotating force
[5] _richochets_: bounces off

Pearson Edexcel International GCSE English Anthology
Issue 1 — April 2016 © Pearson Education Limited 2016

40   wall with my arm in tow, tearing the skin off the lateral side of my forearm. Then
      silence.

      My disbelief paralyzes me temporarily as I stare at the sight of my arm vanishing into an
      implausibly small gap between the fallen boulder and the canyon wall. Within moments,
      my nervous system's pain response overcomes the initial shock. Good God, my hand.
45   The flaring agony throws me into a panic. I grimace and growl … My mind commands my
      body, 'Get your hand out of there!' I yank my arm three times in a naive attempt to pull
      it out. But I'm stuck.

      Anxiety has my brain tweaking; searing-hot pain shoots from my wrist up my arm. I'm
      frantic, and I cry out … My desperate brain conjures up a probably apocryphal[6] story in
50   which an adrenaline-stoked mom lifts an overturned car to free her baby. I'd give it even
      odds that it's made up, but I do know for certain that *right now*, while my body's
      chemicals are raging at full flood, is the best chance I'll have to free myself with brute
      force. I shove against the large boulder, heaving against it, pushing with my left hand,
      lifting with my knees pressed under the rock. I get good leverage with the aid of a
55   twelve-inch shelf in front of my feet. Standing on that, I brace my thighs under the
      boulder and thrust upward repeatedly, grunting, 'Come on…move!' Nothing.

Annotations:

passive voice

he's no in control and shock → scared about what happened to his hand.

(short sentence) *→ he's now very panic and options are limited*

(dialogue punctuation)

one word sentence

his option is limited
He's being desperate

(confident)
- Mathematical language
- Expert terminology
- Dependent clause
- Assured tone
- active voice

(panicked)
- Dialogue
- Exclamation marks
- verb choice
- Short sentences

(Lost control)
- passive voice
- personification
- Temporal marker
- Listing

→ he pt carefully planned out everything that he going to do / *he was very sure that he can do it*

Line 32: instinctively ↓ *but.*

→ it shows that he can't control himself anymore even he planned out everything *(reacted to the situation)*

Shows the situation that are very dangerous.

the stone is very close to him. not controlling himself.

---

[6] *apocryphal*: doubtful, untrue

Young and dyslexic? You've got it going on, Benjamin Zephaniah

This article was published in *The Guardian* online, Friday 2 October 2015, and is adapted from Zephaniah's contribution to *Creative, Successful, Dyslexic* (Jessica Kingsley, 2015).

As a child I suffered, but learned to turn dyslexia to my advantage, to see the world more creatively. We are the architects, we are the designers.

I'm of the generation where teachers didn't know what dyslexia was. The big problem
5 with the education system then was that there was no compassion, no understanding and no humanity. I don't look back and feel angry with the teachers. The ones who wanted to have an individual approach weren't allowed to. The idea of being kind and thoughtful and listening to problems just wasn't done: the past is a different kind of country.

At school my ideas always contradicted the teachers'. I remember one teacher saying
10 that human beings sleep for one-third of their life and I put my hand up and said, "If there's a God isn't that a design fault? If you've built something, you want efficiency. If I was God I would have designed sleep so we could stay awake. Then good people could do one-third more good in the world."

The teacher said, 'Shut up, stupid boy. Bad people would do one-third more bad.' I
15 thought I'd put in a good idea. I was just being creative. She also had a point, but the thing was, she called me stupid for even thinking about it.

I remember a teacher talking about Africa and the 'local savages' and I would say, 'Who are you to talk about savages?' She would say, 'How dare you challenge me?' – and that would get me into trouble.

20 Once, when I was finding it difficult to engage with writing and had asked for some help, a teacher said, 'It's all right. We can't all be intelligent, but you'll end up being a good sportsperson, so why don't you go outside and play some football?' I thought, 'Oh great', but now I realise he was stereotyping me.

I had poems in my head even then, and when I was 10 or 11 my sister wrote some of
25 them down for me. When I was 13 I could read very basically but it would be such hard work that I would give up. I thought that so long as you could read how much the banknote was worth, you knew enough or you could ask a mate.

I got thrown out of a lot of schools, the last one at 13. I was expelled partly because of arguing with teachers on an intellectual level and partly for being a rude boy and
30 fighting. I didn't stab anybody, but I did take revenge on a teacher once. I stole his car and drove it into his front garden. I remember him telling us the Nazis weren't that bad. He could say that in the classroom. When I was in borstal I used to do this thing of looking at people I didn't want to be like. I saw a guy who spent all his time sitting stooped over and I thought, 'I don't want to be like that,' so I learned to sit with a
35 straight back. Being observant helped me make the right choices.
A high percentage of the prison population are dyslexic, and a high percentage of the architect population. If you look at the statistics, I should be in prison: a black man brought up on the wrong side of town whose family fell apart, in trouble with the police when I was a kid, unable to read and write, with no qualifications and, on top of that,
40 dyslexic. But I think staying out of prison is about conquering your fears and finding your path in life.

When I go into prisons to talk to people I see men and women who, in intelligence and other qualities, are the same as me. But opportunities opened for me and they missed theirs, didn't notice them or didn't take them.

45 I never thought I was stupid. I didn't have that struggle. If I have someone in front of me who doesn't have a problem reading and writing telling me that black people are savages I just think, 'I'm not stupid – you're the one who's stupid.' I just had self-belief.

For my first book I told my poems to my girlfriend, who wrote them down for me. It really took off, especially within the black community. I wrote 'wid luv' for 'with love'.
50 People didn't think they were dyslexic poems, they just thought I wrote phonetically.

At 21 I went to an adult education class in London to learn to read and write. The teacher told me, 'You are dyslexic,' and I was like, 'Do I need an operation?' She explained to me what it meant and I suddenly thought, 'Ah, I get it. I thought I was going crazy.'

55 I wrote more poetry, novels for teenagers, plays, other books and recorded music. I take poetry to people who do not read poetry. Still now, when I'm writing the word 'knot', I have to stop and think, 'How do I write that?' I have to draw something to let me know what the word is to come back to it later. If I can't spell 'question' I just put a question mark and come back to it later.

60 When I look at a book, the first thing I see is the size of it, and I know that's what it's like for a lot of young people who find reading tough. When Brunel University offered me the job of professor of poetry and creative writing, I knew my students would be officially more educated than me. I tell them, 'You can do this course and get the right grade because you have a good memory – but if you don't have passion, creativity,
65 individuality, there's no point.' In my life now, I find that people accommodate my dyslexia. I can perform my poetry because it doesn't have to be word perfect, but I never read one of my novels in public. When I go to literary festivals I always get an actor to read it out for me. Otherwise all my energy goes into reading the book and the mood is lost.

70 If someone can't understand dyslexia it's their problem. In the same way, if someone oppresses me because of my race I don't sit down and think, 'How can I become white?' It's not my problem, it's theirs and they are the ones who have to come to terms with it. If you're dyslexic and you feel there's something holding you back, just remember: it's not you. In many ways being dyslexic is a natural way to be.

75 What's unnatural is the way we read and write. If you look at a pictorial language like Chinese, you can see the word for a woman because the character looks like a woman. The word for a house looks like a house. It is a strange step to go from that to a squiggle that represents a sound.

So don't be heavy on yourself. And if you are a parent of someone with dyslexia don't
80 think of it as a defect. Dyslexia is not a measure of intelligence: you may have a genius on your hands. Having dyslexia can make you creative. If you want to construct a sentence and can't find the word you are searching for, you have to think of a way to write round it. This requires being creative and so your 'creativity muscle' gets bigger.

Kids come up to me and say, 'I'm dyslexic too,' and I say to them, 'Use it to your
85 advantage, see the world differently. Us dyslexic people, we've got it going on – we are the architects. We are the designers.' It's like these kids are proud to be like me and if that helps them, that is great. I didn't have that as a child. I say to them, 'Bloody non-dyslexics ... who do they think they are?'

From *A Game of Polo with a Headless Goat*, Emma Levine

Levine travelled throughout Asia researching and filming unusual sports. In this passage she writes about a donkey race in Karachi, Pakistan.

We drove off to find the best viewing spot, which turned out to be the crest of the hill so we could see the approaching race. I asked the lads if we could join in the 'Wacky Races' and follow the donkeys, and they loved the idea. 'We'll open the car boot, you climb inside and point your camera towards the race. As the donkeys overtake us, we'll join

5 the cars.' 'But will you try and get to the front?' 'Oh yes, that's no problem.'

The two lads who had never been interested in this Karachi sport were suddenly fired up with enthusiasm. We waited for eternity on the brow of the hill, me perched in the boot with a zoom lens pointing out. Nearly one hour later I was beginning to feel rather silly when the only action was a villager on a wobbly bicycle, who nearly fell off as he cycled

10 past and gazed around at us.

Several vehicles went past, and some donkey-carts carrying spectators. 'Are they coming?' we called out to them. 'Coming, coming,' came the reply. I was beginning to lose faith in its happening, but the lads remained confident.

Just as I was assuming that the race had been cancelled, we spotted two approaching

15 donkey-carts in front of a cloud of fumes and dust created by some fifty vehicles roaring up in their wake. As they drew nearer, Yaqoob revved up the engine and began to inch the car out of the lay-by. The two donkeys were almost dwarfed by their entourage[1]; but there was no denying their speed — the Kibla donkey is said to achieve speeds of up to 40 kph, and this looked close. The two were neck-and-neck, their jockeys perched on

20 top of the tiny carts using their whips energetically, although not cruelly.

The noise of the approaching vehicles grew; horns tooting, bells ringing, and the special rattles used just for this purpose (like maracas, a metal container filled with dried beans). Men standing on top of their cars and vans, hanging out of taxis and perched on lorries, all cheered and shouted, while the vehicles jostled to get to the front of the

25 convoy.

Yaqoob chose exactly the right moment to edge out of the road and swerve in front of the nearest car, finding the perfect place to see the two donkeys and at the front of the vehicles. This was Formula One without rules, or a city-centre rush hour gone anarchic; a complete flouting of every type of traffic rule and common sense.

30 Our young driver relished this unusual test of driving skills. It was survival of the fittest, and depended upon the ability to cut in front of a vehicle with a sharp flick of the steering wheel (no lane discipline here); quick reflexes to spot a gap in the traffic for a couple of seconds; nerves of steel, and an effective horn. There were two races — the motorized spectators at the back; in front, the two donkeys, still running close and

35 amazingly not put off by the uproar just behind them. Ahead of the donkeys, oncoming traffic — for it was a main road — had to dive into the ditch and wait there until we had passed. Yaqoob loved it. We stayed near to the front, his hand permanently on the horn and his language growing more colourful with every vehicle that tried to cut in front. …

The road straightened and levelled, and everyone picked up speed as we neared the end

40 of the race. But just as they were reaching the finishing line, the hospital gate, there was a near pile-up as the leading donkey swerved, lost his footing and he and the cart tumbled over. The race was over.

---

[1] *entourage:* a group of people attending or surrounding a person

Pearson Edexcel International GCSE English Anthology
Issue 1 — April 2016 © Pearson Education Limited 2016

And then the trouble began. I assumed the winner was the one who completed the race but it was not seen that way by everyone. Apart from the two jockeys and 'officials'
45 (who, it turned out, were actually monitoring the race) there were over a hundred punters who had all staked money on the race, and therefore had strong opinions. Some were claiming that the donkey had fallen because the other one had been ridden too close to him. Voices were raised, fists were out and tempers rising. Everyone gathered around one jockey and official, while the bookmakers were trying to insist that the race
50 should be re-run.

Yaqoob and Iqbal were nervous of hanging around a volatile situation. They agreed to find out for me what was happening ordering me to stay inside the car as they were swallowed up by the crowd. They emerged sometime later. 'It's still not resolved,' said Iqbal, 'but it's starting to get nasty. I think we should leave.' As we drove away, Yaqoob
55 reflected on his driving skills. 'I really enjoyed that,' he said as we drove off at a more sedate pace. 'But I don't even have my licence yet because I'm underage!'

They both found this hilarious, but I was glad he hadn't told me before; an inexperienced, underage driver causing a massive pile-up in the middle of the high-stakes donkey race could have caused problems.

From *Beyond the Sky and the Earth: A Journey into Bhutan*, Jamie Zeppa

When Zeppa was 24 years old she left Canada to teach in Bhutan. This memoir grew out of an essay she wrote about her early days in the country.

Mountains all around, climbing up to peaks, rolling into valleys, again and again. Bhutan is all and only mountains. I know the technical explanation for the landscape, landmass meeting landmass, the Indian subcontinent colliding into Asia thirty or forty million years ago, but I cannot imagine it. It is easier to picture a giant child gathering earth in great
5   armfuls, piling up rock, pinching mud into ridges and sharp peaks, knuckling out little valleys and gorges, poking holes for water to fall through.

It is my first night in Thimphu, the capital, a ninety-minute drive from the airport in Paro. It took five different flights over four days to get here, from Toronto to Montreal, to Amsterdam to New Delhi to Calcutta to Paro. I am exhausted, but I cannot sleep.
10 From my simple, pine-paneled room at the Druk Sherig hotel, I watch mountains rise to meet the moon. I used to wonder what was on the other side of mountains, how the landscape resolved itself beyond the immediate wall in front of you. Flying in from the baked-brown plains of India this morning, I found out: on the other side of mountains are mountains, more mountains and more mountains again. The entire earth below us
15 was a convulsion of crests and gorges and wind-sharpened pinnacles. Just past Everest, I caught a glimpse of the Tibetan plateau, the edge of a frozen desert 4,500 meters above sea level. Thimphu's altitude is about half of that but even here, the winter air is thin and dry and very cold.

The next morning, I share breakfast of instant coffee, powdered milk, plasticky white
20 bread and flavorless[1] red jam in the hotel with two other Canadians who have signed on to teach in Bhutan for two years. Lorna has golden brown hair, freckles and a no non-sense, home-on-the-farm demeanor[2] that is frequently chattered by her tingling laughter and stories of the wild characters that populate her life in Saskatchewan. Sasha from British Columbia is slight and dark, with an impish smile. After breakfast, we have a brief
25 meeting with Gordon, the field director of the WUSC program in Bhutan, and then walk along the main road of Thimphu. Both Lorna and Sasha have traveled[3] extensively; Lorna trekked all over Europe and northern Africa and Sasha worked for a year in an orphanage in Bombay. They are both ecstatic about Bhutan so far, and I stay close to them, hoping to pick up some of their enthusiasm.

30 Although Thimphu's official population is 20,000, it seems even smaller. It doesn't even have traffic lights. Blue-suited policemen stationed at two intersections along the main street direct the occasional truck or landcruiser using incomprehensible but graceful hand gestures. The buildings all have the same pitched roof, trefoil windows and heavy beams painted with lotus flowers, jewels and clouds. One-storied shops with wooden-
35 shuttered windows open onto the street. They seem to be selling the same things: onions, rice, milk powder, dried fish, plastic buckets and metal plates, quilts and packages of stale, soft cookies from India—Bourbon Biscuits, Coconut Crunchies and the hideously colored[4] Orange Cream Biscuits. There are more signs of the outside world than I had expected: teenagers in acid washed jeans, Willie Nelson's greatest hits after
40 the news in English on the Bhutan Broadcasting Service, a Rambo poster in a bar. Overall, these signs of cultural infiltration are few, but they are startling against the Bhutanese-ness of everything else.

---

[1] *flavorless*: American spelling of *flavourless*
[2] *demeanor*: American spelling of *demeanour*
[3] *traveled*: American spelling of *travelled*
[4] *colored*: American spelling of *coloured*

The town itself looks very old, with cracked sidewalks and faded paintwork, but Gordon told us that it didn't exist thirty-odd years ago. Before the sixties, when the third king
45   decided to make it the capital, it was nothing but rice paddies, a few farm houses, and a *dzong*—one of the fortresses that are scattered throughout the country. Thimphu is actually new. "Thimphu will look like New York to you when you come back after a year in the east," he said.

At the end of the main road is Tashichho Dzong, the seat of the Royal Government of
50   Bhutan, a grand, whitewashed, red-roofed, golden-tipped fortress, built in the traditional way, without blueprints or nails. Beyond, hamlets are connected by footpaths, and terraced fields, barren now, climb steadily from the river and merge into forest. Thimphu will never look like New York to me, I think.

The Bhutanese are a very handsome people, 'the best built race of men I ever saw,'
55   wrote emissary George Bogle on his way to Tibet in 1774, and I find I agree. Of medium height and sturdily built, they have beautiful aristocratic faces with dark, almond-shaped eyes, high cheekbones and gentle smiles. Both men and women wear their black hair short. The women wear a *kira*, a brightly striped, ankle-length dress and the men a *gho*, a knee-length robe that resembles a kimono, except that the top part is exceptionally
60   voluminous. The Bhutanese of Nepali origin tend to be taller, with sharper features and darker complexions. They too wear the gho and kira. People look at us curiously, but they do not seem surprised at our presence. Although we see few other foreigners in town, we know they are here. Gordon said something this morning about Thimphu's small but friendly 'ex-pat' community.

65   When we stop and ask for directions at a hotel, the young man behind the counter walks with us to the street, pointing out the way, explaining politely in impeccable English. I search for the right word to describe the people, for the quality that impresses me most—dignity, unselfconsciousness, good humor[5], grace—but can find no single word to hold all of my impressions.

70   In Thimphu, we attended a week-long orientation session with twelve other Irish, British, Australian and New Zealand teachers new to Bhutan. Our first lessons, in Bhutanese history, are the most interesting. Historical records show that waves of Tibetan immigrants settled in Bhutan sometime before the tenth century, but the area is thought to have been inhabited long before that. In the eighth century, the Indian saint
75   Padmasambhava brought Buddhism to the area, where it absorbed many elements of Bon, the indigenous shamanist religion. The new religion took hold but was not a unifying force. The area remained a collection of isolated valleys, each ruled by its own king. When the Tibetan lama Ngawang Namgyel arrived in 1616, he set about unifying the valleys under one central authority and gave the country the name Druk Yul,
80   meaning Land of the Thunder Dragon. Earlier names for Bhutan are just as beautiful—the Tibetans knew the country as the Southern Land of Medicinal Herbs and the South Sandalwood Country. Districts within Bhutan were even more felicitously-named: Rainbow District of Desires, Lotus Grove of the Gods, Blooming Valley of Luxuriant Fruits, the Land of Longing and Silver Pines. Bhutan, the name by which the country
85   came to be known to the outside world, is thought to be derived from *Bhotanta*, meaning the 'end of Tibet' or from the Sanskrit *Bhu-uttan*, meaning 'highlands'.

While the rest of Asia was being overrun by Europeans of varying hue but similar cry, only a handful of Westerners found their way into Bhutan. Two Portuguese Jesuits came to call in 1627, and six British missions paid brief but cordial visits from the late 1700s
90   until the middle of the next century. Relations with the British took a nasty turn during the disastrous visit of Ashley Eden in 1864. Eden, who had gone to sort out a small

---

[5] humor: American spelling of *humour*

problem of the Bhutanese raids on the British territory, had his back slapped, his hair pulled, and his face rubbed with wet dough, and was then forced to sign an outrageous treaty that led to a brief war between the British and the Bhutanese. Considering the

95   consolidated British empire in the south, and the Great Game being played out in the north between the colonial powers, Bhutan's preservation of its independence was remarkable. I am full of admiration for this small country that has managed to look after itself so well.

From *H is for Hawk*, Helen Macdonald

When Macdonald's father died suddenly of a heart attack, Macdonald was devastated. An experienced falconer, she adopted a goshawk to distract her from her grief. In this extract Macdonald meets her hawk for the first time.

'We'll check the ring numbers against the Article 10s,' he explained, pulling a sheaf of yellow paper from his rucksack and unfolding two of the official forms that accompany captive-bred rare birds throughout their lives. 'Don't want you going home with the wrong bird.'

5   We noted the numbers. We stared down at the boxes, at their parcel-tape handles, their doors of thin plywood and hinges of carefully tied string. Then he knelt on the concrete, untied a hinge on the smaller box and squinted into its dark interior. A sudden *thump* of feathered shoulders and the box shook as if someone had punched it, hard, from within. 'She's got her hood off,' he said, and frowned. That light, leather hood was to keep the

10 hawk from fearful sights. Like us.

Another hinge untied. Concentration. Infinite caution. Daylight irrigating the box. Scratching talons, another thump. And another. *Thump.* The air turned syrupy, slow, flecked with dust. The last few seconds before a battle. And with the last bow pulled free, he reached inside, and amidst a whirring, chaotic clatter of wings and feet and

15 talons and a high-pitched twittering and it's all happening at once, the man pulls an enormous, enormous hawk out of the box and in a strange coincidence of world and deed a great flood of sunlight drenches us and everything is brilliance and fury. The hawk's wings, barred and beating, the sharp fingers of her dark-tipped primaries cutting the air, her feathers raised like the scattered quills of a fretful porpentine[1]. Two

20 enormous eyes. My heart jumps sideways. She is a conjuring trick. A reptile. A fallen angel. A griffon from the pages of an illuminated bestiary[2]. Something bright and distant, like gold falling through water. A broken marionette[3] of wings, legs and light-splashed feathers. She is wearing jesses[4], and the man holds them. For one awful, long moment she is hanging head-downward, wings open, like a turkey in a butcher's shop,

25 only her head is turned right-way-up and she is seeing more than she has ever seen before in her whole short life. Her world was an aviary no larger than a living room. Then it was a box. But now it is this; and she can see *everything*: the point-source glitter on the waves, a diving cormorant a hundred yards out; pigment flakes under wax on the lines of parked cars; far hills and the heather on them and miles and miles of sky where

30 the sun spreads on dust and water and illegible things moving in it that are white scraps of gulls. Everything startling and new-stamped on her entirely astonished brain.

Through all this the man was perfectly calm. He gathered up the hawk in one practised movement, folding her wings, anchoring her broad feathered back against his chest, gripping her scaled yellow legs in one hand. 'Let's get that hood back on,' he said tautly.

35 There was concern in his face. It was born of care. This hawk had been hatched in an incubator, had broken from a frail bluish eggshell into a humid perspex box, and for the first few days of her life this man had fed her with scraps of meat held in a pair of tweezers, waiting patiently for the lumpen, fluffy chick to notice the food and eat, her new neck wobbling with the effort of keeping her head in the air. All at once I loved this

40 man, and fiercely. I grabbed the hood from the box and turned to the hawk. Her beak was open, her hackles raised; her wild eyes were the colour of sun on white paper, and they stared because the whole world had fallen into them at once. One, two, three. I

---

[1] *porpentine*: a type of porcupine animal
[2] *bestiary*: a (medieval) descriptive passage on various kinds of animals
[3] *marionette*: a puppet worked by strings
[4] *jesses*: a short leather strap fastened to the leg

Pearson Edexcel International GCSE English Anthology
Issue 1 — April 2016 © Pearson Education Limited 2016

tucked the hood over her head. There was a brief intimation of a thin, angular skull under her feathers, of an alien brain fizzing and fusing with terror, then I drew the

45 braces closed. We checked the ring numbers against the form.

It was the wrong bird. This was the younger one. The smaller one. This was not my hawk.

Oh.

So we put her back and opened the other box, which was meant to hold the larger, older

50 bird. And dear God, it did. Everything about this second hawk was different. She came out like a Victorian melodrama: a sort of madwoman in the attack. She was smokier and darker and much, much bigger, and instead of twittering, she wailed; great, awful gouts of sound like a thing in pain, and the sound was unbearable. *This is my hawk*, I was telling myself and it was all I could do to breathe. She too was bareheaded, and I

55 grabbed the hood from the box as before. But as I brought it up to her face I looked into her eyes and saw something blank and crazy in her stare. Some madness from a distant country. I didn't recognise her. *This isn't my hawk.* The hood was on, the ring numbers checked, the bird back in the box, the yellow form folded, the money exchanged, and all I could think was, *But this isn't my hawk.* Slow panic. I knew what I had to say, and it

60 was a monstrous breach of etiquette. 'This is really awkward,' I began. 'But I really liked the first one. Do you think there's any chance I could take that one instead . . .?' I tailed off. His eyebrows were raised. I started again, saying stupider things: 'I'm sure the other falconer would like the larger bird? She's more beautiful than the first one, isn't she? I know this is out of order, but I … Could I? Would it be all right, do you think?' And on

65 and on, a desperate, crazy barrage of incoherent appeals.

I'm sure nothing I said persuaded him more than the look on my face as I said it. A tall, white faced woman with wind-wrecked hair and exhausted eyes was pleading with him on a quayside, hands held out as if she were in a seaside production of Medea. Looking at me he must have sensed that my stuttered request wasn't a simple one. That there

70 was something behind it that was very important. There was a moment of total silence.

From *Chinese Cinderella*, Adeline Yen Mah

Growing up in a wealthy family in 1950s Hong Kong, Mah should have had an enviable childhood, but she was rejected by her dominating stepmother and despised by her brothers and sisters. She was sent to a boarding school and left there. In this extract from her autobiography she relates one of the few occasions when she went home.

Time went by relentlessly and it was Saturday again. Eight weeks more and it would be the end of term … in my case perhaps the end of school forever.

Four of us were playing Monopoly. My heart was not in it and I was losing steadily. Outside it was hot and there was a warm wind blowing. The radio warned of a possible

5 typhoon the next day. It was my turn and I threw the dice. As I played, the thought of leaving school throbbed at the back of my mind like a persistent toothache.

'Adeline!' Ma-mien Valentino was calling.

'You can't go now,' Mary protested. 'For once I'm winning. One, two, three, four. Good! You've landed on my property. Thirty-five dollars, please. Oh, good afternoon, Mother

10 Valentino!'

We all stood up and greeted her.

'Adeline, didn't you hear me call you? Hurry up downstairs! Your chauffeur is waiting to take you home!'

Full of foreboding, I ran downstairs as in a nightmare, wondering who had died this time.

15 Father's chauffeur assured me everyone was healthy.

'Then why are you taking me home?' I asked.

'How should *I* know?' he answered defensively, shrugging his shoulders. 'Your guess is as good as mine. They give the orders and I carry them out.'

During the short drive home, my heart was full of dread and I wondered what I had done

20 wrong. Our car stopped at an elegant villa at mid-level, halfway up the hill between the peak and the harbour.

'Where are we?' I asked foolishly.

'Don't you know anything?' the chauffeur replied rudely. 'This is your new home. Your parents moved here a few months ago.'

25 'I had forgotten,' I said as I got out.

Ah Gum opened the door. Inside, it was quiet and cool.

'Where is everyone?'

'Your mother is out playing bridge. Your two brothers and Little Sister are sunbathing by the swimming-pool. Your father is in his room and wants to see you as soon as you get

30 home.'

'See me in his room?' I was overwhelmed by the thought that I had been summoned by Father to enter the Holy of Holies — a place to which I had never been invited. Why? …

Timidly, I knocked on the door. Father was alone, looking relaxed in his slippers and bathrobe, reading a newspaper. He smiled as I entered and I saw he was in a happy

35 mood. I breathed a small sigh of relief at first but became uneasy when I wondered why he was being so nice, thinking, Is this a giant ruse on his part to trick me? Dare I let my guard down?

'Sit down! Sit down!' He pointed to a chair. 'Don't look so scared. Here, take a look at this! They're writing about someone we both know, I think.'

40   He handed me the day's newspaper and there, in one corner, I saw my name ADELINE YEN in capital letters prominently displayed.

'It was announced today that 14-year-old Hong Kong schoolgirl ADELINE JUN-LING YEN of Sacred Heart Canossian School, Caine Road, Hong Kong, has won first prize in the International Play-writing Competition held in London, England, for the 1951—1952

45   school year. It is the first time that any local Chinese student from Hong Kong has won such a prestigious event. Besides a medal, the prize comes with a cash reward of FIFTY ENGLISH POUNDS. Our sincere congratulations, ADELINE YEN, for bringing honour to Hong Kong. We are proud of you'.

Is it possible? Am I dreaming? Me, the winner?

50   'I was going up the lift this morning with my friend C.Y. Tung when he showed me this article and asked me, "Is the winner Adeline Jun-ling Yen related to you? The two of you have the same uncommon last name." Now C.Y. himself has a few children about your age but so far none of them has won an international literary prize, as far as I know. So I was quite pleased to tell him you are my daughter. Well done!'

55   He looked radiant. For once, he was proud of me. In front of his revered colleague, C.Y. Tung, a prominent fellow businessman also from Shanghai, I had given him face. I thought, Is this the big moment I have been waiting for? My whole being vibrated with all the joy in the world. I only had to stretch out my hand to reach the stars.

'Tell me, how did you do it?' he continued. 'How come *you* won?'

60   'Well, the rules and regulations were so very complicated. One really has to be dedicated just to understand what they want. Perhaps I was the only one determined enough to enter and there were no other competitors!'

He laughed approvingly. 'I doubt it very much but that's a good answer.'

'Please, Father,' I asked boldly, thinking it was now or never. 'May I go to university in
65   England too, just like my brothers?'

'I do believe you have potential. Tell me, what would you study?'

My heart gave a giant lurch as it dawned on me that he was agreeing to let me go. How marvellous it was simply to be alive! Study? I thought. Going to England is like entering heaven. Does it matter what you do after you get to heaven?

70   But Father was expecting an answer. What about creative writing? After all, I had just won first prize in an international writing competition!

'I plan to study literature. I'll be a writer.'

'Writer!' he scoffed. 'You are going to starve! What language are you going to write in and who is going to read your writing? Though you may think you're an expert in both
75   Chinese and English, your Chinese is actually rather elementary. As for your English, don't you think the native English speakers can write better than you?'

I waited in silence. I did not wish to contradict him.

'You will go to England with Third Brother this summer and you will go to medical school. After you graduate, you will specialise in obstetrics. Women will always be having
80   babies. Women patients prefer women doctors. You will learn to deliver their babies. That's a foolproof profession for you. Don't you agree?'

Agree? Of course I agreed. Apparently, he had it all planned out. As long as he let me go to university in England, I would study anything he wished. How did that line go in Wordsworth's poem? *Bliss was it in that dawn to be alive.*

85   'Father, I shall go to medical school in England and become a doctor. Thank you very, very much.'

Pearson Edexcel International GCSE English Anthology
Issue 1 — April 2016 © Pearson Education Limited 2016

Part 2: Paper 2 Section A Poetry and Prose texts

Pearson Edexcel International GCSE English Anthology
Issue 1 — April 2016 © Pearson Education Limited 2016

Disabled

He sat in a wheeled chair, waiting for dark,
And shivered in his ghastly suit of grey,
Legless, sewn short at elbow. Through the park
Voices of boys rang saddening like a hymn,
5   Voices of play and pleasures after day,
Till gathering sleep had mothered them from him.

About this time Town used to swing so gay
When glow-lamps budded in the light-blue trees,
And girls glanced lovelier as the air grew dim —
10   In the old times, before he threw away his knees.
Now he will never feel again how slim
Girls' waists are, or how warm their subtle hands;
All of them touch him like some queer disease.

There was an artist silly for his face,
15   For it was younger than his youth, last year.
Now, he is old; his back will never brace;
He's lost his colour very far from here,
Poured it down shell-holes till the veins ran dry,
And half his lifetime lapsed in the hot race,
20   And leap of purple spurted from his thigh.

One time he liked a blood-smear down his leg,
After the matches, carried shoulder-high.
It was after football, when he'd drunk a peg,
He thought he'd better join. — He wonders why.
25   Someone had said he'd look a god in kilts,
That's why; and maybe, too, to please his Meg;
Aye, that was it, to please the giddy jilts
He asked to join. He didn't have to beg;

Smiling they wrote his lie; aged nineteen years.
30   Germans he scarcely thought of; all their guilt,
And Austria's, did not move him. And no fears
Of Fear came yet. He thought of jewelled hilts
For daggers in plaid socks; of smart salutes;
And care of arms; and leave; and pay arrears;
35   *Esprit de corps*;[1] and hints for young recruits.
And soon, he was drafted out with drums and cheers.

Some cheered him home, but not as crowds cheer Goal.
Only a solemn man who brought him fruits
Thanked him; and then inquired about his soul.

40   Now, he will spend a few sick years in Institutes,
And do what things the rules consider wise,
And take whatever pity they may dole.
Tonight he noticed how the women's eyes
Passed from him to the strong men that were whole.
45   How cold and late it is! Why don't they come
And put him into bed? Why don't they come?

Wilfred Owen

---

[1] *esprit de corps*: a feeling of pride in the group to which one belongs (French)

'Out, Out –'

The buzz saw snarled and rattled in the yard
And made dust and dropped stove-length sticks of wood,
Sweet-scented stuff when the breeze drew across it.
And from there those that lifted eyes could count
5   Five mountain ranges one behind the other
Under the sunset far into Vermont.
And the saw snarled and rattled, snarled and rattled,
As it ran light, or had to bear a load.
And nothing happened: day was all but done.
10   Call it a day, I wish they might have said
To please the boy by giving him the half hour
That a boy counts so much when saved from work.
His sister stood beside them in her apron
To tell them "Supper." At the word, the saw,
15   As if to prove saws knew what supper meant,
Leaped out at the boy's hand, or seemed to leap—
He must have given the hand. However it was,
Neither refused the meeting. But the hand!
The boy's first outcry was a rueful laugh,
20   As he swung toward them holding up the hand,
Half in appeal, but half as if to keep
The life from spilling. Then the boy saw all—
Since he was old enough to know, big boy
Doing a man's work, though a child at heart—
25   He saw all spoiled. "Don't let him cut my hand off—
The doctor, when he comes. Don't let him, sister!"
So. But the hand was gone already.
The doctor put him in the dark of ether.
He lay and puffed his lips out with his breath.
30   And then—the watcher at his pulse took fright.
No one believed. They listened at his heart.
Little—less—nothing!—and that ended it.
No more to build on there. And they, since they
Were not the one dead, turned to their affairs.

Robert Frost

Pearson Edexcel International GCSE English Anthology
Issue 1 — April 2016 © Pearson Education Limited 2016

An Unknown Girl

In the evening bazaar
studded with neon
an unknown girl
is hennaing[1] my hand.
5 She squeezes a wet brown line
from a nozzle.
She is icing my hand,
which she steadies with hers
on her satin-peach knee.
10 In the evening bazaar
for a few rupees
an unknown girl
is hennaing my hand.
As a little air catches
15 my shadow-stitched kameez[2]
a peacock spreads its lines
across my palm.
Colours leave the street
float up in balloons.
20 Dummies in shop-fronts
tilt and stare
with their Western perms.
Banners for Miss India 1993,
for curtain cloth
25 and sofa cloth
canopy me.
I have new brown veins.
In the evening bazaar
very deftly
30 an unknown girl
is hennaing my hand.
I am clinging
to these firm peacock lines
like people who cling
35 to the sides of a train.
Now the furious streets
are hushed.
I'll scrape off
the dry brown lines
40 before I sleep,
reveal soft as a snail trail
the amber bird beneath.
It will fade in a week.
When India appears and reappears
45 I'll lean across a country
with my hands outstretched
longing for the unknown girl
in the neon bazaar.

Moniza Alvi

---

[1] *hennaing:* the art of body decoration using a plant die
[2] *kameez:* loose fitting tunic

The Bright Lights of Sarajevo

After the hours that Sarajevans pass
queuing with empty canisters of gas
to get the refills they wheel home in prams,
or queuing for the precious meagre grams
5   of bread they're rationed to each day,
and often dodging snipers on the way,
or struggling up sometimes eleven flights
of stairs with water, then you'd think the nights
of Sarajevo would be totally devoid
10   of people walking streets Serb shells destroyed,
but tonight in Sarajevo that's just not the case –
the young go walking at stroller's pace,
black shapes impossible to mark
as Muslim, Serb or Croat in such dark,
15   in unlit streets you can't distinguish who
calls bread *hjleb* or *hleb* or calls it *kruh.*
All take the evening air with stroller's stride
no torches guide them, but they don't collide
except as one of the flirtatious ploys
20   when a girl's dark shape is fancied by a boy's.
Then the tender radar of the tone of voice
shows by its signals she approves his choice.
Then match or lighter to a cigarette
to check in her eyes if he's made progress yet.

25   And I see a pair who've certainly progressed
beyond the tone of voice and match-flare test
and he's about, I think, to take her hand
and leave her away from where they stand
on two shell scars, where, in 1992
30   Serb mortars massacred the breadshop queue
and blood-dunked crusts of shredded bread
lay on this pavement with the broken dead.
And at their feet in holes made by the mortar
that caused the massacre, now full of water
35   from the rain that's poured down half the day,
though now even the smallest clouds have cleared away,
leaving the Sarajevo star-filled evening sky
ideally bright and clear for bomber's eye,
in those two rain-full shell-holes the boy sees
40   fragments of the splintered Pleiades,
sprinkled on those death-deep, death-dark wells
splashed on the pavement by Serb mortar shells.

The dark boy-shape leads dark girl-shape away
to share one coffee in a candlelit café
45   until the curfew, and he holds in her hand
behind AID flour-sacks refilled with sand.

Tony Harrison

Pearson Edexcel International GCSE English Anthology
Issue 1 — April 2016 © Pearson Education Limited 2016

Still I Rise

You may write me down in history
With your bitter, twisted lies,
You may trod me in the very dirt
But still, like dust, I'll rise.

5   Does my sassiness upset you?
Why are you beset with gloom?
'Cause I walk like I've got oil wells
Pumping in my living room.

Just like moons and like suns,
10   With the certainty of tides,
Just like hopes springing high,
Still I'll rise.

Did you want to see me broken?
Bowed head and lowered eyes?
15   Shoulders falling down like teardrops,
Weakened by my soulful cries?

Does my haughtiness offend you?
Don't you take it awful hard
'Cause I laugh like I've got gold mines
20   Diggin' in my own backyard.

You may shoot me with your words,
You may cut me with your eyes,
You may kill me with your hatefulness,
But still, like air, I'll rise.

25   Does my sexiness upset you?
Does it come as a surprise
That I dance like I've got diamonds
At the meeting of my thighs?

Out of the huts of history's shame
30   I rise
Up from a past that's rooted in pain
I rise
I'm a black ocean, leaping and wide,
Welling and swelling I bear in the tide.

35   Leaving behind nights of terror and fear
I rise
Into a daybreak that's wondrously clear
I rise
Bringing the gifts that my ancestors gave,
40   I am the dream and the hope of the slave.
I rise
I rise
I rise.

Maya Angelou

The Story of an Hour

Knowing that Mrs. Mallard was afflicted with a heart trouble, great care was taken to break to her as gently as possible the news of her husband's death.

It was her sister Josephine who told her, in broken sentences; veiled hints that revealed in half concealing. Her husband's friend Richards was there, too, near her. It was he who
5 had been in the newspaper office when intelligence of the railroad disaster was received, with Brently Mallard's name leading the list of "killed." He had only taken the time to assure himself of its truth by a second telegram, and had hastened to forestall any less careful, less tender friend in bearing the sad message.

She did not hear the story as many women have heard the same, with a paralyzed
10 inability to accept its significance. She wept at once, with sudden, wild abandonment, in her sister's arms. When the storm of grief had spent itself she went away to her room alone. She would have no one follow her.

There stood, facing the open window, a comfortable, roomy armchair. Into this she sank, pressed down by a physical exhaustion that haunted her body and seemed to reach into
15 her soul.

She could see in the open square before her house the tops of trees that were all aquiver with the new spring life. The delicious breath of rain was in the air. In the street below a peddler was crying his wares. The notes of a distant song which some one was singing reached her faintly, and countless sparrows were twittering in the eaves.

20 There were patches of blue sky showing here and there through the clouds that had met and piled one above the other in the west facing her window.

She sat with her head thrown back upon the cushion of the chair, quite motionless, except when a sob came up into her throat and shook her, as a child who has cried itself to sleep continues to sob in its dreams.

25 She was young, with a fair, calm face, whose lines bespoke repression and even a certain strength. But now there was a dull stare in her eyes, whose gaze was fixed away off yonder on one of those patches of blue sky. It was not a glance of reflection, but rather indicated a suspension of intelligent thought.

There was something coming to her and she was waiting for it, fearfully. What was it?
30 She did not know; it was too subtle and elusive to name. But she felt it, creeping out of the sky, reaching toward her through the sounds, the scents, the color that filled the air.

Now her bosom rose and fell tumultuously. She was beginning to recognize this thing that was approaching to possess her, and she was striving to beat it back with her will-- as powerless as her two white slender hands would have been. When she abandoned
35 herself a little whispered word escaped her slightly parted lips. She said it over and over under her breath: "free, free, free!" The vacant stare and the look of terror that had followed it went from her eyes. They stayed keen and bright. Her pulses beat fast, and the coursing blood warmed and relaxed every inch of her body.

She did not stop to ask if it were or were not a monstrous joy that held her. A clear and
40 exalted perception enabled her to dismiss the suggestion as trivial. She knew that she would weep again when she saw the kind, tender hands folded in death; the face that had never looked save with love upon her, fixed and gray and dead. But she saw beyond that bitter moment a long procession of years to come that would belong to her absolutely. And she opened and spread her arms out to them in welcome.

Pearson Edexcel International GCSE English Anthology
Issue 1 — April 2016 © Pearson Education Limited 2016

45   There would be no one to live for during those coming years; she would live for herself. There would be no powerful will bending hers in that blind persistence with which men and women believe they have a right to impose a private will upon a fellow-creature. A kind intention or a cruel intention made the act seem no less a crime as she looked upon it in that brief moment of illumination.

50   And yet she had loved him--sometimes. Often she had not. What did it matter! What could love, the unsolved mystery, count for in the face of this possession of self-assertion which she suddenly recognized as the strongest impulse of her being!

"Free! Body and soul free!" she kept whispering.

Josephine was kneeling before the closed door with her lips to the keyhole, imploring for
55   admission. "Louise, open the door! I beg; open the door--you will make yourself ill. What are you doing, Louise? For heaven's sake open the door."

"Go away. I am not making myself ill." No; she was drinking in a very elixir of life through that open window.

Her fancy was running riot along those days ahead of her. Spring days, and summer
60   days, and all sorts of days that would be her own. She breathed a quick prayer that life might be long. It was only yesterday she had thought with a shudder that life might be long.

She arose at length and opened the door to her sister's importunities. There was a feverish triumph in her eyes, and she carried herself unwittingly like a goddess of
65   Victory. She clasped her sister's waist, and together they descended the stairs. Richards stood waiting for them at the bottom.

Some one was opening the front door with a latchkey. It was Brently Mallard who entered, a little travel-stained, composedly carrying his grip-sack and umbrella. He had been far from the scene of the accident, and did not even know there had been one. He
70   stood amazed at Josephine's piercing cry; at Richards' quick motion to screen him from the view of his wife.

When the doctors came they said she had died of heart disease--of the joy that kills.

Kate Chopin

The Necklace

She was one of those pretty, delightful girls who, apparently by some error of Fate, get themselves born the daughters of very minor civil servants. She had no dowry, no expectations, no means of meeting some rich, important man who would understand, love, and marry her. So she went along with a proposal made by a junior clerk in the
5   Ministry of Education.

She dressed simply, being unable to afford anything better, but she was every whit as unhappy as any daughter of good family who has come down in the world. Women have neither rank nor class, and their beauty, grace, and charm do service for birthright and connections. Natural guile, instinctive elegance, and adaptability are what determines
10   their place in the hierarchy, and a girl of no birth to speak of may easily be the equal of any society lady.

She was unhappy all the time, for she felt that she was intended for a life of refinement and luxury. She was made unhappy by the run-down apartment they lived in, the peeling walls, the battered chairs, and the ugly curtains. Now all this, which any other
15   woman of her station might never even have noticed, was torture to her and made her very angry. The spectacle of the young Breton peasant girl who did the household chores stirred sad regrets and impossible fancies. She dreamed of silent antechambers hung with oriental tapestries, lit by tall, bronze candelabras, and of two tall footmen in liveried breeches asleep in the huge armchairs, dozing in the heavy heat of a stove. She
20   dreamed of great drawing-rooms dressed with old silk, filled with fine furniture which showed off trinkets beyond price, and of pretty little parlours, filled with perfumes and just made for intimate talk at five in the afternoon with one's closest friends who would be the most famous and sought-after men of the day whose attentions were much coveted and desired by all women.

25   When she sat down to dinner at the round table spread with a three-day-old cloth, facing her husband who always lifted the lid of the soup-tureen and declared delightedly: 'Ah! Stew! Splendid! There's nothing I like better than a nice stew...', she dreamed of elegant dinners, gleaming silverware, and tapestries which peopled the walls with mythical characters and strange birds in enchanted forests; she dreamed of exquisite dishes
30   served on fabulous china plates, of pretty compliments whispered into willing ears and received with Sphinx-like smiles over the pink flesh of a trout or the wings of a hazel hen.

She had no fine dresses, no jewellery, nothing. And that was all she cared about; she felt that God had made her for such things. She would have given anything to be
35   popular, envied, attractive, and in demand.

She had a friend who was rich, a friend from her convent days, on whom she never called now, for she was always so unhappy afterwards. Sometimes, for days on end, she would weep tears of sorrow, regret, despair, and anguish.

One evening her husband came home looking highly pleased with himself. In his hand he
40   brandished a large envelope.

'Look,' he said, 'I've got something for you.'

She tore the paper flap eagerly and extracted a printed card bearing these words:

    'The Minister of Education and Madame Georges Ramponneau request the pleasure
    of the company of Monsieur and Madame Loisel at the Ministry Buildings on the
45   evening of 18 January.'

Instead of being delighted as her husband had hoped, she tossed the invitation peevishly onto the table and muttered: 'What earthly use is that to me?'

'But, darling, I thought you'd be happy. You never go anywhere and it's an opportunity, a splendid opportunity! I had the dickens of a job getting hold of an invite. Everybody's

50   after them; they're very much in demand and not many are handed out to us clerks. You'll be able to see all the big nobs there.'

She looked at him irritably and said shortly: 'And what am I supposed to wear if I do go?'

He had not thought of that. He blustered: 'What about the dress you wear for the
55   theatre? It looks all right to me …' The words died in his throat. He was totally disconcerted and dismayed by the sight of his wife who had begun to cry. Two large tears rolled slowly out of the corners of her eyes and down towards the sides of her mouth.

'What's up?' he stammered. 'What's the matter?'

60   Making a supreme effort, she controlled her sorrows and, wiping her damp cheeks, replied quite calmly: 'Nothing. It's just that I haven't got anything to wear and consequently I shan't be going to any reception. Give the invite to one of your colleagues with a wife who is better off for clothes than I am.'

He was devastated. He went on: 'Oh come on, Mathilde. Look, what could it cost to get
65   something suitable that would do for other occasions, something fairly simple?'

She thought for a few moments, working out her sums but also wondering how much she could decently ask for without drawing an immediate refusal and pained protests from her husband who was careful with his money. Finally, after some hesitation, she said: 'I can't say precisely, but I daresay I could get by on four hundred francs.'

70   He turned slightly pale, for he had been setting aside just that amount to buy a gun and finance hunting trips the following summer in the flat landscape around Nanterre with a few friends who went shooting larks there on Sundays. But he said: 'Very well. I'll give you your four hundred francs. But do try and get a decent dress.'

The day of the reception drew near and Madame Loisel appeared sad, worried, anxious.
75   Yet all her clothes were ready. One evening her husband said: 'What's up? You haven't half been acting funny these last few days.'

She replied: 'It vexes me that I haven't got a single piece of jewellery, not one stone, that I can put on. I'll look like a church mouse. I'd almost as soon not go to the reception.'

80   'Wear a posy,' he said. 'It's all the rage this year. You could get two or three magnificent roses for ten francs.'

She was not convinced. 'No. …There's nothing so humiliating as to look poor when you're with women who are rich.'

But her husband exclaimed: 'You aren't half silly! Look, go and see your friend, Madame
85   Forestier, and ask her to lend you some jewellery. You know her well enough for that.'

She gave a delighted cry: 'You're right! I never thought of that!'

The next day she called on her friend and told her all about her problem. Madame Forestier went over to a mirror-fronted wardrobe, took out a large casket, brought it over, unlocked it, and said to Madame Loisel: 'Choose whatever you like.'

90   At first she saw bracelets, then a rope of pearls and a Venetian cross made of gold and diamonds admirably fashioned. She tried on the necklaces in the mirror, and could hardly bear to take them off and give them back. She kept asking: 'Have you got anything else?'

'Yes, of course. Just look. I can't say what sort of thing you'll like best.'

95   All of a sudden, in a black satinwood case, she found a magnificent diamond necklace, and her heart began to beat with immoderate desire. Her hands shook as she picked it

up. She fastened it around her throat over her high-necked dress and sat looking at herself in rapture. Then, diffidently, apprehensively, she asked: 'Can you lend me this? Nothing else. Just this.'

100   'But of course.'

She threw her arms around her friend, kissed her extravagantly, and then ran home, taking her treasure with her.

The day of the reception arrived. Madame Loisel was a success. She was the prettiest woman there, elegant, graceful, radiant, and wonderfully happy. All the men looked at
105   her, enquired who she was, and asked to be introduced. All the cabinet secretaries and under-secretaries wanted to waltz with her. She was even noticed by the Minister himself.

She danced ecstatically, wildly, intoxicated with pleasure, giving no thought to anything else, swept along on her victorious beauty and glorious success, and floating on a cloud
110   of happiness composed of the homage, admiration, and desire she evoked and the kind of complete and utter triumph which is so sweet to a woman's heart.

She left at about four in the morning. Since midnight her husband had been dozing in a small, empty side-room with three other men whose wives were having an enjoyable time.

115   He helped her on with her coat which he had fetched when it was time to go, a modest, everyday coat, a commonplace coat violently at odds with the elegance of her dress. It brought her down to earth, and she would have preferred to slip away quietly and avoid being noticed by the other women who were being arrayed in rich furs. But Loisel grabbed her by the arm: 'Wait a sec. You'll catch cold outside. I'll go and get a cab.'

120   But she refused to listen and ran quickly down the stairs. When they were outside in the street, there was no cab in sight. They began looking for one, hailing all the cabbies they saw driving by in the distance.

They walked down to the Seine in desperation, shivering with cold. There, on the embankment, they at last found one of those aged nocturnal hackney cabs which only
125   emerge in Paris after dusk, as if ashamed to parade their poverty in the full light of day. It bore them back to their front door in the rue des Martyrs, and they walked sadly up to their apartment. For her it was all over, while he was thinking that he would have to be at the Ministry at ten.

Standing in front of the mirror, she took off the coat she had been wearing over her
130   shoulders, to get a last look at herself in all her glory. Suddenly she gave a cry. The necklace was no longer round her throat!

Her husband, who was already half undressed, asked: 'What's up?'

She turned to him in a panic: 'I ... I ... Madame Forestier's necklace ... I haven't got it!'

He straightened up as if thunderstruck: 'What? ... But ... You can't have lost it!'

135   They looked in the pleats of her dress, in the folds of her coat, and in her pockets. They looked everywhere. They did not find it.

'Are you sure you still had it when you left the ballroom?' he asked.

'Yes, I remember fingering it in the entrance hall.'

'But if you'd lost it in the street, we'd have heard it fall. So it must be in the cab.'

140   'That's right. That's probably it. Did you get his number?'

'No. Did you happen to notice it?'

'No.'

They looked at each other in dismay. Finally Loisel got dressed again. 'I'm going to go back the way we came,' he said, 'to see if I can find it.' He went out. She remained as she was, still wearing her evening gown, not having the strength to go to bed, sitting disconsolately on a chair by the empty grate, her mind a blank.

Her husband returned at about seven o'clock. He had found nothing.

He went to the police station, called at newspaper offices where he advertised a reward, toured the cab companies, and tried anywhere where the faintest of hopes led him. She waited for him all day long in the same distracted condition, thinking of the appalling catastrophe which had befallen them.

Loisel came back that evening, hollow-cheeked and very pale. He had not come up with anything.

'Look,' he said, 'you'll have to write to your friend and say you broke the catch on her necklace and you are getting it repaired. That'll give us time to work out what we'll have to do.'

She wrote to his dictation.

A week later they had lost all hope.

Loisel, who had aged five years, said: 'We'll have to start thinking about replacing the necklace.'

The next day they took the case in which it had come and called on the jeweller whose name was inside. He looked through his order book.

'It wasn't me that sold the actual necklace. I only supplied the case.'

After this, they trailed round jeweller's shops, looking for a necklace just like the other one, trying to remember it, and both ill with worry and anxiety.

In a shop in the Palais Royal they found a diamond collar which they thought was identical to the one they were looking for. It cost forty thousand francs. The jeweller was prepared to let them have it for thirty-six.

They asked him not to sell it for three days. And they got him to agree to take it back for thirty-four thousand if the one that had been lost turned up before the end of February.

Loisel had eighteen thousand francs which his father had left him. He would have to borrow the rest.

He borrowed the money, a thousand francs here, five hundred there, sometimes a hundred and as little as sixty. He signed notes, agreed to pay exorbitant rates of interest, resorted to usurers and the whole tribe of moneylenders. He mortgaged the rest of his life, signed papers without knowing if he would ever be able to honour his commitments, and then, sick with worry about the future, the grim poverty which stood ready to pounce, and the prospect of all the physical privation and mental torture ahead, he went round to the jeweller's to get the new necklace with the thirty-six thousand francs which he put on the counter.

When Madame Loisel took it round, Madame Forestier said in a huff: 'You ought really to have brought it back sooner. I might have needed it.'

She did not open the case, as her friend had feared she might. If she had noticed the substitution, what would she have thought? What would she have said? Would she not have concluded she was a thief?

Then began for Madame Loisel the grindingly horrible life of the very poor. But quickly and heroically, she resigned herself to what she could not alter: their appalling debt would have to be repaid. She was determined to pay. They dismissed the maid. They moved out of their apartment and rented an attic room.

190   She became used to heavy domestic work and all kinds of ghastly kitchen chores. She washed dishes, wearing down her pink nails on the greasy pots and saucepans. She washed the dirty sheets, shirts, and floorcloths by hand and hung them up to dry on a line; each morning she took the rubbish down to the street and carried the water up, pausing for breath on each landing. And, dressed like any working-class woman, she

195   shopped at the fruiterer's, the grocer's, and the butcher's, with a basket over her arm, haggling, frequently abused and always counting every penny.

Each month they had to settle some accounts, renew others, and bargain for time.

Her husband worked in the evenings doing accounts for a shopkeeper and quite frequently sat up into the early hours doing copying work at five sous[1] a page.

200   They lived like this for ten years.

By the time ten years had gone by, they had repaid everything, with not a penny outstanding, in spite of the extortionate conditions and including the accumulated interest.

Madame Loisel looked old now. She had turned into the battling, hard, uncouth

205   housewife who rules working-class homes. Her hair was untidy, her skirts were askew, and her hands were red. She spoke in a gruff voice and scrubbed floors on her hands and knees. But sometimes, when her husband had gone to the office, she would sit by the window and think of that evening long ago when she had been so beautiful and so admired.

210   What might not have happened had she not lost the necklace? Who could tell? Who could possibly tell? Life is so strange, so fickle! How little is needed to make or break us!

One Sunday, needing a break from her heavy working week, she went out for a stroll on the Champs-Élysées[2]. Suddenly she caught sight of a woman pushing a child in a pram. It was Madame Forestier, still young, still beautiful, and still attractive.

215   Madame Loisel felt apprehensive. Should she speak to her? Yes, why not? Now that she had paid in full, she would tell her everything. Why not? She went up to her.
'Hello, Jeanne.'

The friend did not recognize her and was taken aback at being addressed so familiarly by a common woman in the street. She stammered: 'But … I'm sorry … I don't know …

220   There's some mistake.'

'No mistake. I'm Madame Loisel.'

Her friend gave a cry: 'But my poor Mathilde, how you've changed!'

'Yes, I've been through some hard times since I saw you, very hard times. And it was all on your account.'

225   'On my account? Whatever do you mean?'

'Do you remember that diamond necklace you lent me to go to the reception at the Ministry?'

'Yes. What about it?'

'Well I lost it.'

230   'Lost it? But you returned it to me.'

'No, I returned another one just like it. And we've been paying for it these past ten years. You know, it wasn't easy for us. We had nothing. … But it's over and done with now, and I'm glad.'

---

[1] *sous*: a coin of very small value
[2] *Champs-Élysées*: a famous street in Paris

Pearson Edexcel International GCSE English Anthology
Issue 1 — April 2016 © Pearson Education Limited 2016

Madame Forestier stopped. 'You mean you bought a diamond necklace to replace mine?'

235 'Yes. And you never noticed the difference, did you? They were exactly alike.' And she smiled a proud, innocent smile.

Madame Forestier looked very upset and, taking both her hands in hers, said:

'Oh, my poor Mathilde! But it was only an imitation necklace. It couldn't have been worth much more than five hundred francs! ...'

Guy de Maupassant

Significant Cigarettes (from *The Road Home*)

On the coach, Lev chose a seat near the back and he sat huddled against the window, staring out at the land he was leaving: at the fields of sunflowers scorched by the dry wind, at the pig farms, at the quarries and rivers and at the wild garlic growing green at the edge of the road.

5   Lev wore a leather jacket and jeans and a leather cap pulled low over his eyes and his handsome face was grey-toned from his smoking and in his hands he clutched an old red cotton handkerchief and a dented pack of Russian cigarettes. He would soon be forty-three.

After some miles, as the sun came up, Lev took out a cigarette and stuck it between his
10   lips, and the woman sitting next to him, a plump, contained person with moles like splashes of mud on her face, said quickly: 'I'm sorry, but there is no smoking allowed on this bus.'

Lev knew this, had known it in advance, had tried to prepare himself mentally for the long agony of it. But even an unlit cigarette was a companion – something to hold on to,
15   something that had promise in it – and all he could be bothered to do now was to nod, just to show the woman that he'd heard what she'd said, reassure her that he wasn't going to cause trouble; because there they would have to sit for fifty hours or more, side by side with their separate aches and dreams, like a married couple. They would hear each other's snores and sighs, smell the food and drink each had brought with them,
20   note the degree to which each was fearful or unafraid, make short forays into conversation. And then later, when they finally arrived in London, they would probably separate with barely a word or a look, walk out into a rainy morning, each alone and beginning a new life. And Lev thought how all of this was odd but necessary and already told him things about the world he was travelling to, a world in which he would break his
25   back working – if only that work could be found. He would hold himself apart from other people, find corners and shadows in which to sit and smoke, demonstrate that he didn't need to belong, that his heart remained in his own country.

There were two coach-drivers. These men would take turns to drive and to sleep. There was an on-board lavatory, so the only stops the bus would make would be for gas. At
30   gas stations, the passengers would be able to clamber off, walk a few paces, see wild flowers on a verge, soiled paper among bushes, sun or rain on the road. They might stretch up their arms, put on dark glasses against the onrush of nature's light, look for a clover leaf, smoke and stare at the cars rushing by. Then they would be herded back onto the coach, resume their old attitudes, arm themselves for the next hundred miles,
35   for the stink of another industrial zone, or the sudden gleam of a lake, for rain and sunset and the approach of darkness on silent marshes. There would be times when the journey would seem to have no end.

Sleeping upright was not something Lev was practised in. The old seemed to be able to do it, but forty-two was not yet old. Lev's father, Stefan, sometimes used to sleep
40   upright, in summer, on a hard wooden chair in his lunch break at the Baryn sawmill, with the hot sun falling onto the slices of sausage wrapped in paper on his knee and onto his flask of tea. Both Stefan and Lev could sleep lying down on a mound of hay or on the mossy carpet of a forest. Often, Lev had slept on a rag rug beside his daughter's bed, when she was ill or afraid. And when his wife, Marina, was dying, he'd lain for five nights
45   on an area of linoleum flooring no wider than his outstretched arm, between Marina's hospital bed and a curtain patterned with pink and purple daisies, and sleep had come and gone in a mystifying kind of way, painting strange pictures in Lev's brain that had never completely vanished.

Towards evening, after two stops for gas, the mole-flecked woman unwrapped a hard-
50   boiled egg. She peeled it silently. The smell of the egg reminded Lev of the sulphur springs at Jor, where he'd taken Marina, just in case nature could cure what man had

Pearson Edexcel International GCSE English Anthology
Issue 1 — April 2016 © Pearson Education Limited 2016

given up for lost. Marina had immersed her body obediently in the scummy water, lain there looking at a female stork returning to its high nest, and said to Lev: 'If only we were storks.'

55   'Why d'you say that?' Lev had asked.

'Because you never see a stork dying. It's as though they didn't die.'

If only we were storks.

On the woman's knee a clean cotton napkin was spread and her white hands smoothed it and she unwrapped rye bread and a twist of salt.

60   'My name is Lev,' said Lev.

'My name is Lydia,' said the woman. And they shook hands, Lev's hand holding the scrunched-up kerchief, and Lydia's hand rough with salt and smelling of egg, and then Lev asked: 'What are you planning to do in England?' and Lydia said: 'I have some interviews in London for jobs as a translator.'

65   'That sounds promising.'

'I hope so. I was a teacher of English at School 237 in Yarbl, so my language is very colloquial.'

Lev looked at Lydia. It wasn't difficult to imagine her standing in front of a class and writing words on a blackboard. He said: 'I wonder why you're leaving our country when
70   you had a good job at School 237 in Yarbl?'

'Well,' said Lydia. 'I became very tired of the view from my window. Every day, summer and winter, I looked out at the school yard and the high fence and the apartment block beyond, and I began to imagine I would die seeing these things, and I didn't want this. I expect you understand what I mean?'

75   Lev took off his leather cap and ran his fingers through his thick grey hair. He saw Lydia turn to him for a moment and look very seriously into his eyes.

He said: 'Yes, I understand.'

Then there was a silence, while Lydia ate her hard-boiled egg. She chewed very quietly. When she'd finished the egg, Lev said: 'My English isn't too bad. I took some classes in
80   Baryn, but my teacher told me my pronunciation wasn't very good. May I say some words and you can tell me if I'm pronouncing them correctly?'

'Yes, of course,' said Lydia.

Lev said: 'Lovely. Sorry. I am legal. How much please. Thank you. May you help me.'

'May I help you,' corrected Lydia.

85   'May I help you,' repeated Lev.

'Go on,' said Lydia.

'Stork,' said Lev. 'Stork's nest. Rain. I am lost. I wish for an interpreter. Bee-and-bee.'

'Be-and-be?' said Lydia. 'No, no. You mean "to be, or not to be".'

'No,' said Lev. 'Bee-and-bee. Family hotel, quite cheap.'

90   'Oh, yes, I know. B & B.'

Lev could now see that darkness was falling outside the window and he thought how, in his village, darkness had always arrived in precisely the same way, from the same direction, above the same trees, whether early or late, whether in summer, winter or spring, for the whole of his life. This darkness – particular to that place, Auror – was
95   how, in Lev's heart, darkness would always fall.

And so he told Lydia that he came from Auror, had worked in the Baryn sawmill until it closed two years ago, and since then he'd found no work at all and his family – his mother, his five-year-old daughter and he – had lived off the money his mother made selling jewellery manufactured from tin.

100 'Oh,' said Lydia. 'I think that's very resourceful, to make jewellery from tin.'

'Sure,' said Lev. 'But it isn't enough.'

Tucked into his boot was a small flask of vodka. He extracted the flask and took a long swig. Lydia kept eating her rye bread. Lev wiped his mouth with the red handkerchief and saw his face reflected in the coach window. He looked away. Since the death of
105 Marina, he didn't like to catch sight of his own reflection, because what he always saw in it was his own guilt at still being alive.

'Why did the sawmill at Baryn close?' asked Lydia.

'They ran out of trees,' said Lev.

'Very bad,' said Lydia. 'What other work can you do?'

110 Lev drank again. Someone had told him that in England vodka was too expensive to drink. Immigrants made their own alcohol from potatoes and tap water, and when Lev thought about these industrious immigrants, he imagined them sitting by a coal fire in a tall house, talking and laughing, with rain falling outside the window and red buses going past and a television flickering in a corner of the room. He sighed and said: 'I will do any
115 work at all. My daughter Maya needs clothes, shoes, books, toys, everything. England is my hope.'

Towards ten o'clock, red blankets were given out to the coach passengers, some of whom were already sleeping. Lydia put away the remnants of her meal, covered her body with the blanket and switched on a fierce little light above her under the baggage
120 rack and began reading a faded old paperback, printed in English. Lev saw that the title of her book was The Power and the Glory. His longing for a cigarette had grown steadily since he'd drunk the vodka and now it was acute. He could feel the yearning in his lungs and in his blood, and his hands grew fidgety and he felt a tremor in his legs. How long before the next gas stop? It could be four or five hours. Everyone on the bus would be
125 asleep by then, except him and one of the two drivers. Only they would keep a lonely, exhausting vigil, the driver's body tensed to the moods and alarms of the dark, unravelling road; his own aching for the comfort of nicotine or oblivion – and getting neither.

He envied Lydia, immersed in her English book. Lev knew he had to distract himself with
130 something…. In desperation, he took from his wallet a brand new British twenty-pound note and reached up and switched on his own little reading light and began to examine the note. On one side, the frumpy Queen, E II R, with her diadem, her face grey on a purple ground, and on the other, a man, some personage from the past, with a dark drooping moustache and an angel blowing a trumpet above him and all the angel's
135 radiance falling on him in vertical lines. 'The British venerate their history,' Lev had been told in his English class, 'chiefly because they have never been subjected to Occupation. Only intermittently do they see that some of their past deeds were not good.'

The indicated lifespan of the man on the note was 1857–1934. He looked like a banker, but what had he done to be on a twenty-pound note in the twenty-first century? Lev
140 stared at his determined jaw, squinted at his name written out in a scrawl beneath the wing collar, but couldn't read it. He thought that this was a person who would never have known any other system of being alive but Capitalism. He would have heard the names Hitler and Stalin, but not been afraid – would have had no need to be afraid of anything except a little loss of capital in what Americans called the Crash, when men in
145 New York had jumped out of windows and off roofs. He would have died safely in his bed before London was bombed to ruins, before Europe was torn apart. Right to the end of

Pearson Edexcel International GCSE English Anthology
Issue 1 — April 2016 © Pearson Education Limited 2016

his days, the angel's radiance had probably shone on this man's brow and on his fusty clothes, because it was known across the world: the English were lucky. Well, thought Lev, I'm going to their country now and I'm going to make them share it with me: their
150   infernal luck. I've left Auror and that leaving of my home was hard and bitter, but my time is coming.

Rose Tremain

Whistle and I'll Come to You (from *The Woman in Black*)

During the night the wind rose. As I had lain reading I had become aware of the stronger gusts that blew every so often against the casements. But when I awoke abruptly in the early hours it had increased greatly in force. The house felt like a ship at sea, battered by the gale that came roaring across the open marsh. Windows were rattling everywhere
5   and there was the sound of moaning down all the chimneys of the house and whistling through every nook and cranny.

At first I was alarmed. Then, as I lay still, gathering my wits, I reflected on how long Eel Marsh House had stood here, steady as a lighthouse, quite alone and exposed, bearing the brunt of winter after winter of gales and driving rain and sleet and spray. It was
10   unlikely to blow away tonight. And then, those memories of childhood began to be stirred again and I dwelt nostalgically upon all those nights when I had lain in the warm and snug safety of my bed in the nursery at the top of our family house in Sussex, hearing the wind rage round like a lion, howling at the doors and beating upon the windows but powerless to reach me. I lay back and slipped into that pleasant, trance-like
15   state somewhere between sleeping and waking, recalling the past and all its emotions and impressions vividly, until I felt I was a small boy again.

Then from somewhere, out of that howling darkness, a cry came to my ears, catapulting me back into the present and banishing all tranquillity.

I listened hard. Nothing. The tumult of the wind, like a banshee, and the banging and
20   rattling of the window in its old, ill-fitting frame. Then yes, again, a cry, that familiar cry of desperation and anguish, a cry for help from a child somewhere out on the marsh.

There was no child. I knew that. How could there be? Yet how could I lie here and ignore even the crying of some long-dead ghost?

'Rest in peace,' I thought, but this poor one did not, could not.

25   After a few moments I got up. I would go down into the kitchen and make myself a drink, stir up the fire a little and sit beside it trying, trying to shut out that calling voice for which I could do nothing, and no one had been able to do anything for… how many years?

As I went out onto the landing, Spider the dog following me at once, two things
30   happened together. I had the impression of someone who had just that very second before gone past me on their way from the top of the stairs to one of the other rooms, and, as a tremendous blast of wind hit the house so that it all but seemed to rock at the impact, the lights went out. I had not bothered to pick up my torch from the bedside table and now I stood in the pitch blackness, unsure for a moment of my bearings.

35   And the person who had gone by, and who was now in this house with me? I had seen no one, felt nothing. There had been no movement, no brush of a sleeve against mine, no disturbance of the air, I had not even heard a footstep. I had simply the absolutely certain sense of someone just having passed close to me and gone away down the corridor. Down the short narrow corridor that led to the nursery whose door had been so
40   firmly locked and then, inexplicably, opened.

For a moment, I actually began to conjecture[1] that there was indeed someone – another human being – living here in this house, a person who hid themselves away in that mysterious nursery and came out at night to fetch food and drink and to take the air. Perhaps it was the woman in black? Had Mrs Drablow harboured some reclusive old
45   sister or retainer, had she left behind her a mad friend that no one had known about? My brain span all manner of wild, incoherent fantasies as I tried desperately to provide a rational explanation for the presence I had been so aware of. But then they ceased. There was no living occupant of Eel Marsh House other than myself and Samuel Daily's

---

[1] *conjecture*: an opinion formed on the basis of incomplete information

Pearson Edexcel International GCSE English Anthology
Issue 1 — April 2016 © Pearson Education Limited 2016

50   dog. Whatever was about, whoever I had seen, and heard rocking, and who had passed me by just now, whoever had opened the locked door was not 'real'. No. But what *was* 'real'? At that moment I began to doubt my own reality.

The first thing I must have was a light and I groped my way back across to my bed, reached over it and got my hand to the torch at last, took a step back, stumbled over the dog who was at my heels and dropped the torch. It went spinning away across the
55   floor and fell somewhere by the window with a crash and the faint sound of breaking glass. I cursed but managed, by crawling about on my hands and knees, to find it again and to press the switch. No light came on. The torch had broken.

For a moment I was as near to weeping tears of despair and fear, frustration and tension, as I had ever been since my childhood. But instead of crying I drummed my
60   fists upon the floorboards, in a burst of violent rage, until they throbbed.

It was Spider who brought me to my senses by scratching a little at my arm and then by licking the hand I stretched out to her. We sat on the floor together and I hugged her warm body to me, glad of her, thoroughly ashamed of myself, calmer and relieved, while the wind boomed and roared without, and again and again I heard that child's terrible
65   cry borne on the gusts towards me.

Susan Hill

Night

When I was young, there seemed to be never a childbirth, or a burst appendix, or any other drastic physical event that did not occur simultaneously with a snowstorm. The roads would be closed, there was no question of digging out a car anyway, and some horses had to be hitched up to make their way into town to the hospital. It was just

5   lucky that there were horses still around – in the normal course of events they would have been given up, but the war and gas rationing had changed all that, at least for the time being.

When the pain in my side struck, therefore, it had to do so at about eleven o'clock at night, and a blizzard had to be blowing, and since we were not stabling any horses at the

10   moment, the neighbors'[1] team had to be brought into action to take me to the hospital. A trip of no more than a mile and a half but an adventure all the same. The doctor was waiting, and to nobody's surprise he prepared to take out my appendix. …

So I lay, minus my appendix, for some days looking out a hospital window at the snow sifting in a somber way through some evergreens. I don't suppose it ever crossed my

15   head to wonder how my father was going to pay for this distinction. (I think he sold a woodlot that he had kept when he disposed of his father's farm. He would have hoped to use it for trapping or sugaring. Or perhaps he felt an unmentionable nostalgia.)

Then I went back to school, and enjoyed being excused from physical training for longer than necessary, and one Saturday morning when my mother and I were alone in the

20   kitchen she told me that my appendix had been taken out in the hospital, just as I thought, but it was not the only thing removed. The doctor had seen fit to take it out while he was at it, but the main thing that concerned him was a growth. A growth, my mother said, the size of a turkey's egg.

But don't worry, she said, it's all over now.

25   The thought of cancer never entered my head and she never mentioned it. I don't think there could be such a revelation today without some kind of question, some probing about whether it was or it wasn't. Cancerous or benign – we would want to know at once. The only way I can explain our failure to speak of it was that there must have been a cloud around that word…

30   So I did not ask and wasn't told and can only suppose it was benign or was most skillfully got rid of, for here I am today. And so little do I think of it that all through my life when called upon to list my surgeries, I automatically say or write only "Appendix". …

In the heat of early June I got out of school, having made good enough marks to free me from the final examination. I looked well, I did chores around the house, I read books as

35   usual, nobody knew there was a thing the matter with me.

Now I have to describe the sleeping arrangements in the bedroom occupied by my sister and myself. It was a small room that could not accommodate two single beds side by side, so the solution was a pair of bunk beds, with a ladder in place to help whoever slept in the top bunk climb into bed. That was me. When I had been younger and prone

40   to teasing, I would lift up the corner of my thin mattress and threaten to spit on my little sister lying helpless in the bunk below. Of course my sister – her name was Catherine – was not really helpless. She could hide under her covers, but my game was to watch until suffocation or curiosity drove her out, and at that moment to spit or successfully pretend to spit on her bared face, enraging her.

---

[1] *neighbors*: American spelling of *neighbours*

Pearson Edexcel International GCSE English Anthology
Issue 1 — April 2016 © Pearson Education Limited 2016

45 I was too old for such fooling, certainly too old by this time. My sister was nine when I was fourteen. The relationship between us was always unsettled. When I wasn't tormenting her, teasing her in some asinine way, I would take on the role of sophisticated counsellor or hair-raising storyteller…

    I don't mean to say that I was entirely in control of her, or even that our lives were
50 constantly intertwined. She had her own friends, her own games. …

    In the month June, as I have said, I was free of school and left on my own, as I don't remember being in quite the same way in any other time of my growing-up. I did some chores in the house, but my mother must have been well enough, as yet, to handle most of that work. Or perhaps we had just enough money at the time to hire what she – my
55 mother – would call a maid, though everyone else said hired girl. I don't remember, at any rate, having to tackle any of the jobs that piled up for me in later summers, when I fought quite willingly to maintain the decency of our house. It seems that the mysterious turkey egg must have given me some invalid status, so that I could spend part of the time wandering about like a visitor.

60 Though not trailing any special clouds. Nobody in our family would have got away with that. It was all inward – this uselessness and strangeness I felt. …

    It must have been just that every moment of the day was not filled up with jobs, as it was in summers before and after.

    So maybe that was the reason that I had begun to have trouble getting to sleep. At first,
65 I think, that meant lying wide awake maybe till around midnight and wondering at how wide awake I was, with the rest of the household asleep. I would have read, and got tired in the usual way, and turned out my light and waited. Nobody would have called out to me earlier, telling me to put out my light and get to sleep. For the first time ever (and this too must have marked a special status) I was left to make up my own mind
70 about such a thing.

    It took a while for the house to change from the light of day and from the household lights turned on late into the evening. Leaving behind the general clatter of things to be done, hung up, finished with, it became a stranger place in which people and the work that dictated their lives fell away, their uses for everything around them fell away, all the
75 furniture retreated into itself and no longer existed because of nobody's attention.

    You might think this was a liberation. At first, perhaps it was. The freedom. The strangeness. But as my failure to fall asleep prolonged itself, and as it finally took hold all together until it changed into the dawn, I became more and more disturbed by it. I started saying rhymes, then real poetry, first to make myself go under
80 but then hardly of my own volition. The activity seemed to mock me. I was mocking myself, as the words turned into absurdity, into the silliest random speech.

    I was not myself.

    I had been hearing that said of people now and then, all my life, without thinking what it
85 could mean.

    So who do you think you are, then?

    I had been hearing that too, without attaching to it any real menace, just taking it as a sort of routine jeering.

    Think again.

90   By this time it wasn't sleep I was after. I knew mere sleep wasn't likely. Maybe not even desirable. Something was taking hold of me and it was my business, my hope, to fight it off. I had the sense to do that, but only barely, as it seemed. Whatever it was was trying to tell me to do things, not exactly for any reason but just to see if such acts were possible. It was informing me that motives were not necessary.

95   It was only necessary to give in. How strange. Not out of revenge, or for any normal reason, but just because you had thought of something.

And I did think if it. The more I chased the thought away, the more it came back. No vengeance, no hatred – as I've said, no reason, except something like an utterly cold deep thought that was hardly an urging, more of a contemplation, could take possession
100   of me. I must not even think of it but I did think of it.

The thought was there and hanging in my mind.

The thought that I could strangle my little sister, who was asleep in the bunk below me and whom I loved more than anybody in the world.

I might do it not for jealousy, viciousness, or anger, but because of madness, which
105   could be lying right beside me there in the night. Not a savage madness either, but something that could be almost teasing. A lazy, teasing, half-sluggish suggestion that seemed to have been waiting a long time.

It might be saying why not. Why not try the worst?

The worst. Here in the most familiar place, the room where we had lain for all our lives
110   and thought ourselves most safe. I might do it for no reason I or anybody could understand, except that I could not help it.

The thing to do was to get up, to get myself out of that room and out of the house. I went down the rungs of the ladder and never cast a single look at my sister where she slept. Then quietly down the stairs, nobody stirring, into the kitchen where everything
115   was so familiar to me that I could make my way without a light. The kitchen door was not really locked – I am not even sure that we possessed a key. A chair was pushed under the doorknob so that anybody trying to get in would make a great clatter. A slow careful removal of the chair could be managed without making any noise at all.

After the first night I was able to make my moves without a break, so that I could be
120   outside, as it seemed, within a couple of smooth seconds.

Of course there were no streetlights – we were too far from town.

Everything was larger. The trees around the house were always called by their names – the beech tree, the elm tree, the oak tree, the maples always spoken of in the plural and not differentiated, because they clung together. Now they were all intensely black. So
125   were the white lilac tree (no longer with its blooms) and the purple lilac tree – always called lilac trees not bushes because they had grown too big.

The front and back and side lawns were easy to negotiate because I had mown them myself with the idea of giving us some townlike respectability. …

Back and forth I walked, first close to the house and then venturing here and there as I
130   got to rely on my eyesight and could count on not bumping into the pump handle or the platform that supported the clothesline. The birds began to stir, and then to sing – as if each of them had thought of it separately, up there in the trees. They woke far earlier than I would have thought possible. But soon after those earliest starting songs, there got to be a little whitening in the sky. And suddenly I would be overwhelmed with sleepiness. I
135   went back into the house, where there was suddenly darkness everywhere, and I very properly, carefully , silently, set the tilted chair under the doorknob, and went upstairs without a sound, managing doors and steps with the caution necessary, although I seemed already half asleep. I fell into my pillow, and I woke late – late in our house being around eight o'clock.

140 I would remember everything then, but it was so absurd – the bad part of it indeed was so absurd – that I could get rid of it fairly easily. My brother and sister had gone off to their classes in the public school, but their dishes were still on the table, a few bits of puffed rice floating in the excess milk.

Absurd.

145 When my sister got home from school we would swing in the hammock, one of us at either end.

It was in that hammock that I spent much of the days, which possibly accounted for my not getting to sleep at night. And since I did not speak of my night difficulties, nobody came up with the simple information that I'd be better off getting more action during the

150 day.

My troubles returned with the night, of course. The demons got hold of me again. I knew enough soon to get up and out of my bunk without pretending that things would get better and that I would in fact go to sleep if I tried hard enough. I made my way as carefully out of the house as I had done before. I became able to find my way around

155 more easily; even the inside of the rooms became more visible to me and yet more strange. …

The east wall of the kitchen had no windows in it but it had a door opening on a stoop where we stood to hang out the heavy wet washing, and haul it in when it was dry and smelling all fresh and congratulatory, from white sheets to dark heavy overalls.

160 At that stoop, I sometimes halted in my night walks. I never sat down but it eased me to look towards town, maybe just to inhale the sanity of it. All the people getting up before long, having their shops to go to, their doors to unlock and milk bottles to take inside, their busyness.

One night – I can't say whether it could be the twentieth or the twelfth or only the eighth

165 or the ninth that I had got up and walked – I got a sense, too late for me to change my pace, that there was somebody around the corner. There was somebody waiting there and I could do nothing but walk right on. I would be caught if I turned back, and it would be worse that way than to be confronted.

Who was it? Nobody but my father. He too sitting on the stoop looking towards town and

170 that improbable faint light. He was dressed in his day clothes – dark work pants, the next thing to overalls but not quite, and dark, rough shirt and boots. He was smoking a cigarette. One he rolled himself, of course. Maybe the cigarette smoke had alerted me to another presence, though it's possible that in those days the smell of tobacco smoke was everywhere, inside buildings and out, so there was no way to notice it.

175 He said good morning, in what might have seemed a natural way except that there was nothing natural about it. We weren't accustomed to giving such greetings in our family. There was nothing hostile about this – it was just thought unnecessary, I suppose, when we would see each other off and on all day.

I said good morning back. And it must have really been getting towards morning or my

180 father would not have been dressed for a day's work in that way. The sky may have been whitening but hidden still between the heavy trees. The birds singing, too. I had taken to staying away from my bunk till later and later, even though I didn't get comfort from doing so as I had at first. The possibilities that had once inhabited only the bedroom, the bunk beds, were taking up the corners everywhere.

185 Now that I come to think of it, why wasn't my father in his overalls? He was dressed as if he had to go into town for something, first thing in the morning.

I could not continue walking, the whole rhythm of it had been broken.

'Having trouble sleeping?' he said.

190 My impulse was to say no, but then I thought of the difficulties of explaining that I was just walking around, so I said yes.

He said that was often the case on summer nights.

'You go to bed tired out and then just as you think you're falling asleep you're wide awake. Isn't that the way?'

I said yes.

195 I knew now that he had not heard me getting up and walking around on just this one night. The person whose livestock was on the premises, whose earnings such as they were lay all close by, and who kept a handgun in his desk drawer, was certainly going to stir at the slightest creeping on the stairs and the easiest turning of the knob.

I am not sure what conversation he meant to follow then, as regards to my being awake.
200 He seems to have declared wakefulness to be a nuisance, but was that to be all? I certainly did not intend to tell him more. If he had given the slightest intimation that he knew there was more, if he'd even hinted that he had come here intending to hear it, I don't think he'd have got anything out of me at all. I had to break the silence out of my own will, saying that I could not sleep. I had to get out of bed and walk.

205 Why was that?

I did not know.

Not bad dreams?

No.

'Stupid question,' he said. 'You wouldn't get chased out of your bed on account of good
210 dreams.'

He let me wait to go on, he didn't ask anything. I meant to back off but I kept talking. The truth was told with only the slightest modification.

When I spoke of my little sister I said that I was afraid I would hurt her. I believed that would be enough, that he would know enough of what I meant.

215 'Strangle her,' I said then. I could not stop myself after all.

Now I could not unsay it, I could not go back to the person I had been before.

My father had heard it. He had heard that I thought myself capable of, for no reason, strangling little Catherine in her sleep.

He said, 'Well.'

220 Then he said not to worry. He said, 'People have those kinds of thoughts sometimes.'

He said this quite seriously and without any sort of alarm or jumpy surprise. People have these kinds of thoughts or fears if you like, but there's no real worry about it, no more than a dream, you could say.

He did not say, specifically, that I was in no danger of doing such a thing. He seemed
225 more to be taking it for granted that such a thing could not happen. An effect of the ether, he said. Ether they gave you in the hospital. No more sense than a dream. It could not happen, in the way that a meteor could not hit our house (of course it could, but the likelihood of its doing so put it in the category of couldn't).

He did not blame me though, for thinking if it. Did not wonder at me, was what he said.

230 There were other things he could have said. He could have questioned me further about my attitude to my little sister or my dissatisfactions with my life in general. If this were happening today, he might have made an appointment for me to see a psychiatrist. (I think that is what I might have done for a child, a generation and an income further on.)

235 The fact is, what he did worked as well. It set me down, but without either mockery or alarm, in the world we were living in.

People have thoughts they'd sooner not have. It happens in life.

If you live long enough as a parent nowadays, you discover that you have made mistakes you didn't bother to know about along with the ones you do know about all too well. You are somewhat humbled at heart, sometimes disgusted with yourself. I don't 240 think my father felt anything like this. I do know that if I had ever taxed him, with his use on me of the razor strap or his belt, he might have said something about liking or lumping it. Those strappings, then, would have stayed in his mind, if they stayed at all, as no more than the necessary and adequate curbing of a mouthy child's imagining that she should rule the roost.

245 'You thought you were too smart,' was what he might have given as his reason for the punishments, and indeed you heard that often in those times, with the smartness figuring as an obnoxious imp that had to have the sass beaten out of him. Otherwise there was the risk of him growing up thinking he was smart. Or her, as the case might be.

250 However, on that breaking morning he gave me just what I needed to hear and what I was even to forget about soon enough.

I have thought that he was maybe in his better work clothes because he had a morning appointment to go to the bank, to learn, not to his surprise, that there was no extension to his loan. He had worked as hard as he could but the market was not going to turn 255 around and he had to find a new way of supporting us and paying off what we owed at the same time. Or he may have found out that there was a name for my mother's shakiness and that it was not going to stop. Or that he was in love with an impossible woman.

Never mind. From then on I could sleep.

Alice Munro

Part 3: Paper 1 Section A Poetry

If—

If you can keep your head when all about you
    Are losing theirs and blaming it on you,
If you can trust yourself when all men doubt you,
    But make allowance for their doubting too;
5   If you can wait and not be tired by waiting,
    Or being lied about, don't deal in lies,
Or being hated, don't give way to hating,
    And yet don't look too good, nor talk too wise:

If you can dream — and not make dreams your master;
10   If you can think — and not make thoughts your aim;
If you can meet with Triumph and Disaster
    And treat those two impostors just the same;
If you can bear to hear the truth you've spoken
    Twisted by knaves to make a trap for fools,
15   Or watch the things you gave your life to, broken,
    And stoop and build 'em up with worn-out tools:

If you can make one heap of all your winnings
    And risk it on one turn of pitch-and-toss,
And lose, and start again at your beginnings
20   And never breathe a word about your loss;
If you can force your heart and nerve and sinew
    To serve your turn long after they are gone,
And so hold on when there is nothing in you
    Except the Will which says to them: 'Hold on!'

25   If you can talk with crowds and keep your virtue,
    Or walk with Kings — nor lose the common touch,
If neither foes nor loving friends can hurt you,
    If all men count with you, but none too much;
If you can fill the unforgiving minute
30   With sixty seconds' worth of distance run,
Yours is the Earth and everything that's in it,
    And — which is more — you'll be a Man, my son!

Rudyard Kipling

Prayer Before Birth

I am not yet born; O hear me.
Let not the bloodsucking bat or the rat or the stoat or the
    club-footed ghoul come near me.

I am not yet born, console me.
5   I fear that the human race may with tall walls wall me,
    with strong drugs dope me, with wise lies lure me,
        on black racks rack me, in blood-baths roll me.

I am not yet born; provide me
With water to dandle me, grass to grow for me, trees to talk
10   to me, sky to sing to me, birds and a white light
      in the back of my mind to guide me.

I am not yet born; forgive me
For the sins that in me the world shall commit, my words
    when they speak me, my thoughts when they think me,
15   my treason engendered by traitors beyond me,
        my life when they murder by means of my
          hands, my death when they live me.

I am not yet born; rehearse me
In the parts I must play and the cues I must take when
20   old men lecture me, bureaucrats hector me, mountains
      frown at me, lovers laugh at me, the white
        waves call me to folly and the desert calls
          me to doom and the beggar refuses
            my gift and my children curse me.

25   I am not yet born; O hear me,
Let not the man who is beast or who thinks he is God
    come near me.

I am not yet born; O fill me
With strength against those who would freeze my
30   humanity, would dragoon me into a lethal automaton,
      would make me a cog in a machine, a thing with
        one face, a thing, and against all those
          who would dissipate my entirety, would
            blow me like thistledown hither and
35   thither or hither and thither
              like water held in the
                hands would spill me.

Let them not make me a stone and let them not spill me.
Otherwise kill me.

Louis MacNeice

Pearson Edexcel International GCSE English Anthology
Issue 1 — April 2016 © Pearson Education Limited 2016

Blessing

The skin cracks like a pod.
There never is enough water.

Imagine the drip of it,
the small splash, echo
5   in a tin mug,
the voice of a kindly god.

Sometimes, the sudden rush
of fortune. The municipal pipe bursts,
silver crashes to the ground
10   and the flow has found
a roar of tongues. From the huts,
a congregation : every man woman
child for streets around
butts in, with pots,
15   brass, copper, aluminium,
plastic buckets,
frantic hands,

and naked children
screaming in the liquid sun,
20   their highlights polished to perfection,
flashing light,
as the blessing sings
over their small bones.

Imtiaz Dharker

Search For My Tongue

You ask me what I mean
by saying I have lost my tongue.
I ask you, what would you do
if you had two tongues in your mouth,
5   and lost the first one, the mother tongue,
and could not really know the other,
the foreign tongue.
You could not use them both together
even if you thought that way.
10   And if you lived in a place you had to
speak a foreign tongue,
your mother tongue would rot,
rot and die in your mouth
until you had to "spit it out".
15   I thought I spit it out
but overnight while I dream,

મને હતું કે આખ્ખી જીભ આખ્ખી ભાષા,
(munay hutoo kay aakhee jeebh aakhee bhasha)

મેં થૂંકી નાખી છે.
20   (may thoonky nakhi chay)

પરંતુ રાત્રે સ્વપ્નામાં મારી ભાષા પાછી આવે છે.
(parantoo rattray svupnama mari bhasha pachi aavay chay)

ફૂલની જેમ મારી ભાષા મારી જીભ
(foolnee jaim mari bhasha nmari jeebh)

મોઢામાં ખીલે છે.
25   (modhama kheelay chay)

ફૂલની જેમ મારી ભાષા મારી જીભ
(fullnee jaim mari bhasha mari jeebh)

મોઢામાં પાકે છે.
30   (modhama pakay chay)

it grows back, a stump of a shoot
grows longer, grows moist, grows strong veins,
it ties the other tongue in knots,
the bud opens, the bud opens in my mouth,
35   it pushes the other tongue aside.
Everytime I think I've forgotten,
I think I've lost the mother tongue,
it blossoms out of my mouth.

Sujata Bhatt

Half-past Two

Once upon a schooltime
He did Something Very Wrong
(I forget what it was).

And She said he'd done
5   Something Very Wrong, and must
Stay in the school-room till half-past two.

(Being cross, she'd forgotten
She hadn't taught him Time.
He was too scared at being wicked to remind her.)

10   He knew a lot of time: he knew
Gettinguptime, timeyouwereofftime,
Timetogohomenowtime, TVtime,

Timeformykisstime (that was Grantime).
All the important times he knew,
15   But not half-past two.

He knew the clockface, the little eyes
And two long legs for walking,
But he couldn't click its language,

So he waited, beyond onceupona,
20   Out of reach of all the timefors,
And knew he'd escaped for ever

Into the smell of old chrysanthemums on Her desk,
Into the silent noise his hangnail made,
Into the air outside the window, into ever.

25   And then, *My goodness*, she said,
Scuttling in, *I forgot all about you*.
Run along or you'll be late.

So she slotted him back into schooltime,
And he got home in time for teatime,
30   Nexttime, notimeforthatnowtime,

But he never forgot how once by not knowing time,
He escaped into the clockless land for ever,
Where time hides tick-less waiting to be born.

U A Fanthorpe

Pearson Edexcel International GCSE English Anthology
Issue 1 — April 2016 © Pearson Education Limited 2016

Piano

Softly, in the dusk, a woman is singing to me;
Taking me back down the vista of years, till I see
A child sitting under the piano, in the boom of the tingling strings
And pressing the small, poised feet of a mother who smiles as she
5   sings.

In spite of myself, the insidious mastery of song
Betrays me back, till the heart of me weeps to belong
To the old Sunday evenings at home, with winter outside
And hymns in the cozy parlor, the tinkling piano our guide.

10   So now it is vain for the singer to burst into clamor
With the great black piano appassionato. The glamour
Of childish days is upon me, my manhood is cast
Down in the flood of remembrance, I weep like a child for the past.

D H Lawrence

Hide and Seek

Call out. Call loud: 'I'm ready! Come and find me!'
The sacks in the toolshed smell like the seaside.
They'll never find you in this salty dark,
But be careful that your feet aren't sticking out.
5   Wiser not to risk another shout.
The floor is cold. They'll probably be searching
The bushes near the swing. Whatever happens
You mustn't sneeze when they come prowling in.
And here they are, whispering at the door;
10   You've never heard them sound so hushed before.
Don't breathe. Don't move. Stay dumb. Hide in your blindness.
They're moving closer, someone stumbles, mutters;
Their words and laughter scuffle, and they're gone.
But don't come out just yet; they'll try the lane
15   And then the greenhouse and back here again.
They must be thinking that you're very clever,
Getting more puzzled as they search all over.
It seems a long time since they went away.
Your legs are stiff, the cold bites through your coat;
20   The dark damp smell of sand moves in your throat.
It's time to let them know that you're the winner.
Push off the sacks. Uncurl and stretch. That's better!
Out of the shed and call to them: 'I've won!
Here I am! Come and own up I've caught you!'
25   The darkening garden watches. Nothing stirs.
The bushes hold their breath; the sun is gone.
Yes, here you are. But where are they who sought you?

Vernon Scannell

Pearson Edexcel International GCSE English Anthology
Issue 1 — April 2016 © Pearson Education Limited 2016

Sonnet 116 'Let me not to the marriage...'

Let me not to the marriage of true minds
Admit impediments; love is not love
Which alters when it alteration finds,
Or bends with the remover to remove.
5   O no, it is an ever-fixèd mark
That looks on tempests and is never shaken;
It is the star to every wandering bark,
Whose worth's unknown, although his height be taken.
Love's not Time's fool, though rosy lips and cheeks
10   Within his bending sickle's compass come;
Love alters not with his brief hours and weeks,
But bears it out even to the edge of doom.
        If this be error and upon me proved,
        I never writ, nor no man ever loved.

William Shakespeare

La Belle Dame sans Merci

I
O what can ail thee, knight-at-arms,
    Alone and palely loitering?
The sedge has withered from the lake,
5   And no birds sing.

II
Oh what can ail thee, knight-at-arms,
    So haggard and so woe-begone?
The squirrel's granary is full,
10   And the harvest's done.

III
I see a lily on thy brow,
    With anguish moist and fever-dew,
And on thy cheek a fading rose
15   Fast withereth too.

IV
I met a lady in the meads,
    Full beautiful — a faery's child,
Her hair was long, her foot was light,
20   And her eyes were wild.

V
I made a garland for her head,
    And bracelets too, and fragrant zone;
She looked at me as she did love,
25   And made sweet moan.

VI
I set her on my pacing steed,
    And nothing else saw all day long,
For sidelong would she bend, and sing
30   A faery's song.

VII
She found me roots of relish sweet,
    And honey wild, and manna[1]-dew,
And sure in language strange she said —
35   'I love thee true'.

VIII
She took me to her elfin grot,
    And there she wept and sighed full sore,
And there I shut her wild wild eyes
40   With kisses four.

IX
And there she lullèd me asleep
    And there I dreamed — Ah! woe betide! —
The latest dream I ever dreamt
45   On the cold hill side.

---

[1] *manna*: food from heaven

Pearson Edexcel International GCSE English Anthology
Issue 1 — April 2016 © Pearson Education Limited 2016

X

I saw pale kings, and princes too,
    Pale warriors, death-pale were they all;
They cried — 'La Belle Dame sans Merci
50   Thee hath in thrall!'

XI

I saw their starved lips in the gloam,
    With horrid warning gapèd wide,
And I awoke and found me here,
55   On the cold hill's side.

XII

And this is why I sojourn here
    Alone and palely loitering,
Though the sedge is withered from the lake,
60   And no birds sing.

John Keats

Poem at Thirty-Nine

How I miss my father.
I wish he had not been
so tired
when I was
5   born.

Writing deposit slips and checks
I think of him.
He taught me how.
This is the form,
10   he must have said:
the way it is done.
I learned to see
bits of paper as a way
to escape the life he knew
15   and even in high school
had a savings
account.

He taught me
that telling the truth
20   did not always mean
a beating;
though many of my truths
must have grieved him
before the end.

25   How I miss my father!
He cooked like a person
dancing
in a yoga meditation
and craved the voluptuous
30   sharing
of good food.

Now I look and cook just like him:
my brain light;
tossing this and that
35   into the pot;
seasoning none of my life
the same way twice; happy to feed
whoever strays my way.

He would have grown
40   to admire
the woman I've become:
cooking, writing, chopping wood,
staring into the fire.

Alice Walker

Pearson Edexcel International GCSE English Anthology
Issue 1 — April 2016 © Pearson Education Limited 2016

War Photographer

In his darkroom he is finally alone
with spools of suffering set out in ordered rows.
The only light is red and softly glows,
as though this were a church and he
5   a priest preparing to intone a Mass[1].
Belfast. Beirut. Phnom Penh. All flesh is grass.

He has a job to do. Solutions slop in trays
beneath his hands, which did not tremble then
though seem to now. Rural England. Home again
10   to ordinary pain which simple weather can dispel,
to fields which don't explode beneath the feet
of running children in a nightmare heat.

Something is happening. A stranger's features
faintly start to twist before his eyes,
15   a half-formed ghost. He remembers the cries
of this man's wife, how he sought approval
without words to do what someone must
and how the blood stained into foreign dust.

A hundred agonies in black and white
20   from which his editor will pick out five or six
for Sunday's supplement[2]. The reader's eyeballs prick
with tears between the bath and pre-lunch beers.
From the aeroplane he stares impassively at where
he earns his living and they do not care.

Carol Ann Duffy

---

[1] *mass:* a religious service
[2] *Sunday's supplement:* a regular additional section placed in a Sunday newspaper

The Tyger

Tyger, Tyger, burning bright,
In the forests of the night:
What immortal hand or eye,
Could frame thy fearful symmetry?

5   In what distant deeps or skies
Burnt the fire of thine eyes?
On what wings dare he aspire?
What the hand, dare seize the fire?

And what shoulder, & what art,
10   Could twist the sinews of thy heart?
And when thy heart began to beat,
What dread hand? & what dread feet?

What the hammer? what the chain,
In what furnace was thy brain?
15   What the anvil? what dread grasp,
Dare its deadly terrors clasp!

When the stars threw down their spears
And water'd heaven with their tears:
Did he smile his work to see?
20   Did he who made the Lamb make thee?[1]

Tyger, Tyger burning bright,
In the forests of the night:
What immortal hand or eye,
Dare frame thy fearful symmetry?

William Blake

---

[1] *Did he who made the Lamb make thee?:* God

Pearson Edexcel International GCSE English Anthology
Issue 1 — April 2016 © Pearson Education Limited 2016

My Last Duchess

Ferrara

That's my last Duchess painted on the wall,
Looking as if she were alive. I call
That piece a wonder, now: Frà Pandolf's hands
Worked busily a day, and there she stands.
5   Will't please you sit and look at her? I said
'Frà Pandolf' by design, for never read
Strangers like you that pictured countenance,
The depth and passion of its earnest glance,
But to myself they turned (since none puts by
10   The curtain I have drawn for you, but I)
And seemed as they would ask me, if they durst,
How such a glance came there; so, not the first
Are you to turn and ask thus. Sir, 'twas not
Her husband's presence only, called that spot
15   Of joy into the Duchess' cheek: perhaps
Frà Pandolf chanced to say, 'Her mantle laps
Over my lady's wrist too much,' or 'Paint
Must never hope to reproduce the faint
Half-flush that dies along her throat': such stuff
20   Was courtesy, she thought, and cause enough
For calling up that spot of joy. She had
A heart – how shall I say? – too soon made glad,
Too easily impressed; she liked whate'er
She looked on, and her looks went everywhere.
25   Sir, 'twas all one! My favour at her breast,
The dropping of the daylight in the West,
The bough of cherries some officious fool
Broke in the orchard for her, the white mule
She rode with round the terrace – all and each
30   Would draw from her alike the approving speech,
Or blush, at least. She thanked men, – good! but thanked
Somehow – I know not how – as if she ranked
My gift of a nine-hundred-years-old name
With anybody's gift. Who'd stoop to blame
35   This sort of trifling? Even had you skill
In speech – (which I have not) – to make your will
Quite clear to such an one, and say, 'Just this
Or that in you disgusts me; here you miss,
Or there exceed the mark' – and if she let
40   Herself be lessoned so, nor plainly set
Her wits to yours, forsooth, and made excuse,
– E'en then would be some stooping; and I choose
Never to stoop. Oh, sir, she smiled, no doubt,
Whene'er I passed her; but who passed without
45   Much the same smile? This grew; I gave commands;
Then all smiles stopped together. There she stands
As if alive. Will't please you rise? We'll meet
The company below, then. I repeat,
The Count your master's known munificence

50   Is ample warrant that no just pretence
      Of mine for dowry will be disallowed;
      Though his fair daughter's self, as I avowed
      At starting, is my object. Nay, we'll go
      Together down, sir. Notice Neptune, though,
55   Taming a sea-horse, thought a rarity,
      Which Claus of Innsbruck cast in bronze for me!

Robert Browning

Pearson Edexcel International GCSE English Anthology
Issue 1 — April 2016 © Pearson Education Limited 2016

Half-caste

Excuse me
standing on one leg
I'm half-caste

Explain yuself
5   wha yu mean
when you say half-caste
yu mean when picasso
mix red an green
is a half-caste canvas/
10 explain yuself
wha yu mean
when yu say half-caste
yu mean when light an shadow
mix in de sky
15 is a half-caste weather/
well in dat case
england weather
nearly always half-caste
in fact some o dem cloud
20 half-caste till dem overcast
so spiteful dem dont want de sun pass
ah rass/
explain yuself
wha yu mean
25 when you say half-caste
yu mean Tchaikovsky
sit down at dah piano
an mix a black key
wid a white key
30 is a half-caste symphony/
Explain yuself
wha yu mean
Ah listening to yu wid de keen
half of mih ear
35 Ah lookin at yu wid de keen
half of mih eye
and when I'm introduced to yu
I'm sure you'll understand
why I offer yu half-a-hand
40 an when I sleep at night
I close half-a-eye
consequently when I dream
I dream half-a-dream
an when moon begin to glow
45 I half-caste human being
cast half-a-shadow
but yu must come back tomorrow

wid de whole of yu eye
50   an de whole of yu ear
an de whole of yu mind

an I will tell yu
de other half of my story

John Agard

Do not go gentle into that good night

Do not go gentle into that good night,
Old age should burn and rave at close of day;
Rage, rage against the dying of the light.

Though wise men at their end know dark is right,
5   Because their words had forked no lightning they
Do not go gentle into that good night.

Good men, the last wave by, crying how bright
Their frail deeds might have danced in a green bay,
Rage, rage against the dying of the light.

10   Wild men who caught and sang the sun in flight,
And learn, too late, they grieved it on its way,
Do not go gentle into that good night.

Grave men, near death, who see with blinding sight
Blind eyes could blaze like meteors and be gay,
15   Rage, rage against the dying of the light.

And you, my father, there on the sad height,
Curse, bless, me now with your fierce tears, I pray.
Do not go gentle into that good night.
Rage, rage against the dying of the light.

Dylan Thomas

Remember

Remember me when I am gone away,
Gone far away into the silent land;
    When you can no more hold me by the hand,
Nor I half turn to go yet turning stay.
5   Remember me when no more day by day
    You tell me of our future that you planned:
    Only remember me; you understand
It will be late to counsel then or pray.
Yet if you should forget me for a while
10   And afterwards remember, do not grieve:
    For if the darkness and corruption leave
    A vestige of the thoughts that once I had,
Better by far you should forget and smile
    Than that you should remember and be sad.

Christina Rossetti

Pearson Edexcel International GCSE English Anthology
Issue 1 — April 2016 © Pearson Education Limited 2016

Acknowledgements

We are grateful to the following for permission to reproduce copyright material:

Part 1

Text on p.1 from 'The Danger of a Single Story' by Chimamanda Ngozi Adichie, July 2009, https://www.ted.com/, copyright © Chimamanda Ngozi Adichie 2009. Reproduced by permission of The Wylie Agency (UK) Limited;

Text on p.3 from *A Passage to Africa* by George Alagiah, Abacus, 2007, pp.87-90, copyright © George Alagiah 2001. Reproduced by permission Little, Brown Book Group Limited and the author c/o The Hanbury Agency Ltd, 53 Lambeth Walk, London SE11 6DX. All Rights Reserved;

Text on p.5 from *The Explorer's Daughter* by Kari Herbert, Penguin, 2006, copyright © Kari Herbert 2004. Reproduced by permission of Aitken Alexander Associates Ltd;

An extract on p.7 from "Explorers, or Boys Messing About?" by Steven Morris, *The Guardian*, 28/01/2003, copyright © Guardian News & Media Ltd 2016;

Text on p.9 from *127 hours - Between a Rock and a Hard Place* by Aron Ralston, Simon & Schuster Ltd, 2010, pp.22-24, copyright © Aron Ralston 2004. Reproduced by permission of Simon & Schuster UK Limited and Atria Books, a Division of Simon & Schuster, Inc.

Text on p.11 from "Young and Dyslexic? You've got it going on" by Benjamin Zephaniah, *The Guardian*, 02/10/2015, as adapted from *Creative, Successful, Dyslexic: 23 High Achievers Share Their Stories*, edited by Margaret Rooke, 2015. Reproduced by permission of Jessica Kingsley Publishers;

Text on p.13 from *A Game of Polo with a Headless Goat* by Emma Levine, published by Andre Deutsch, copyright © Emma Levine 2000. Reproduced by permission of Carlton Publishing Group;

Text on p.15 from *Beyond the Sky and the Earth: A Journey into Bhutan* by Jamie Zeppa, Riverhead Books, 2000, copyright © Jamie Zeppa 1999. Reproduced by permission of The McDermid Agency Inc.; Riverhead, an imprint of Penguin Publishing Group, a division of Penguin Random House LLC, and Doubleday Canada, a division of Penguin Random House Canada Limited;

Text on p.18 from *H is for Hawk* by Helen Macdonald, Jonathan Cape, 2014, copyright © Helen Macdonald 2014. Reproduced by permission of The Random House Group Limited; and Grove/Atlantic, Inc.

Text on p.20 from *Chinese Cinderella: The True Story of an Unwanted Daughter* by Adeline Yen Mah, Penguin, 1999, copyright © Adeline Yen Mah 1999. Reproduced with permission of Penguin Books Ltd; Delacorte Press, an imprint of Random House Children's Books, a division of Penguin Random House LLC; and Penguin Random House Australia, All rights reserved.

Part 2

Part 3

Poem on p.54 'Prayer Before Birth' by Louis MacNeice, published in *Collected Poems*, Faber & Faber, 1966, copyright © The Estate of Louis MacNeice, 1966 and 1979. Reproduced by permission of David Higham Associates Limited;

Poem on p.55 'Blessing' by Imtiaz Dharker, published in *Postcards from God*, Bloodaxe Books, 1997. Reproduced by permission of Bloodaxe Books on behalf of the author, www.bloodaxebooks.com;

Poem on p.56 'Search for my Tongue' by Sujata Bhatt published in *Brunizem*, Carcanet, 2007. Reproduced with permission of Carcanet Press Limited;

Poem on p.58 'Half-past two' by U. A. Fanthorpe, published in *New and Collected Poems*, Enitharmon Press, 2010. Reproduced by permission of Dr R V Bailey;

Poem on p.60 'Hide and Seek' by Vernon Scannell, published in *Collected Poems 1950-1993*, Faber & Faber, 2011. Reproduced by permission of the Estate of Vernon Scannell;

Poem on p.64 'Poem at Thirty-Nine' by Alice Walker, published in *Collected Poems: Her Blue Body Everything We Know: Earthling Poems 1965-1990*, Orion. Reproduced by permission of David Higham Associates Limited;

Poem on p.65 'War Photographer' published in *Standing Female Nude* by Carol Ann Duffy, Anvil Press Poetry, 1985, copyright © Carol Ann Duffy. Reproduced by permission of the author c/o Rogers, Coleridge & White Ltd., 20 Powis Mews, London W11 1JN;

Poem on p.69 'Half-caste' by John Agard, copyright © 1996 by John Agard. Reproduced by kind permission of John Agard c/o Caroline Sheldon Literary Agency Ltd;

Poem on p.71 'Do Not Go Gentle into That Good Night' by Dylan Thomas, published in *The Poems of Dylan Thomas* and *The Collected Poems of Dylan Thomas: The New Centenary Edition*, Orion, 2014, copyright © Dylan Thomas 1952 and The Trustees for the copyright of Dylan Thomas. Reproduced by permission of David Higham Associates Limited; and New Directions Publishing Corp.